The Path

Also by Richard Matheson

The Path

A New Look at Reality

Based on the writings of
Harold W. Percival

Richard Matheson

A Tom Doherty Associates Book
New York

THE PATH

Copyright © 1993 by Richard Matheson

This book is printed on acid-free paper.

A Tor Book
Published by Tom Doherty Associates, LLC
175 Fifth Avenue
New York, NY 10010

Tor Books on the World Wide Web:
http://www.tor.com

Tor® is a registered trademark of Tom Doherty Associates, LLC

Library of Congress Cataloguing-in-Publication Data

Matheson, Richard.
  The path : a new look at reality : based on the writings of
Harold W. Percival / Richard Matheson.—1st Tor ed.
    p. cm.
  ISBN 0-312-87057-4 (acid-free paper)
  1. Word Foundation—Doctrines.   I. Title.
BP605.W67M37   1999
299'.93—dc21

                                                              99-12398
                                                                 CIP

First Tor Edition: June 1999

Printed in the United States of America

0 9 8 7 6 5 4 3 2 1

With love

To my wife Ruth Ann,
To my children Bettina, Richard, Ali and Chris,
To my daughters-in-law Marie and Trish,
my sons-in-law Bob and Jon,
And my grandchildren Robert, Lise,
Valerie, Emily, William, Mariel and Kate

For all that they have meant to me
And all that they truly are.

Acknowledgments

With the kind permission of The Word Foundation, Inc., all concepts in this book were taken in their entirety out of the following works by Harold W. Percival: *Thinking and Destiny,*

©1979 The Word Foundation, Inc.,
Democracy Is Self-Government,
©1980 The Word Foundation, Inc.,
Man and Woman and Child,
©1979 The Word Foundation, Inc.
and *The Word Magazine*
©1990 The Word Foundation, Inc.

Interested readers are urged to look for these titles in better bookstores, or else to contact the publisher directly:
The Word Foundation
P.O. Box 180340-R
Dallas, TX 75218 USA

I am indeed grateful to the Foundation, as owner of the copyrights, for its express permission to use Mr. Percival's own words in this book.

—RICHARD MATHESON

Foreword

ALL OF US have experienced the idea that we are part of a broad, cosmological form or process. In this we have the sense of ourselves and, to some degree, of others. As we go through our daily activities we express our connection to the mundane; we eat, drink, laugh, and play, but out of a corner of our minds we wonder—but why? What does it all mean? Where have I come and where do I go?

In this book, the author gradually presents a cosmology through ten walks along a path where the reader participates in a conversation between a mysterious person and an everyman, one of us. Though we have doubts and lack of understanding, we have a passion and openness to learning.

If we can accept the notion that thought, like electricity, has form and physical properties and, like light, can operate over space and time, then we can appreciate and be warmed by the concepts developed in their conversations. Like the everyman, we can grow to appreciate what we have learned about life, death, acting and non-acting and its relationship to our thought and the cosmos, and how this manifests the world we experience. We read the dialogue and grow to appreciate our unique contribution not only to the here and now, but also to the future—all this in the light of what was.

This book was inspired by the teachings of Harold Waldwin Percival, especially his great book, *Thinking and Destiny*. Percival seemed to be born with an ardent metaphysical thirst and in 1892 joined the Theosophical Society and became a staunch member. In the spring of 1893 Percival had an awakening into Cosmic Consciousness. In that instant, according to Percival, "eternities were apprehended. There was no time. Distance and dimensions were not in evidence."

He went on to say that he became conscious of the Presence of Consciousness. He was aware of Consciousness as the Ultimate and Absolute Reality. After this awakening he left the Theosophical Society and all other "teachers." After many more years of study he published *Thinking and Destiny* in 1946. In this vast, dense book, he goes on to define and explain his vision and understanding. Most people need a full year to read and try to comprehend all this great work has to offer.

In this book, *The Path*, Richard Matheson takes a portion of Percival's vast cosmology and presents it as a pleasant, stimulating conversation between friends. Gradually, without quite realizing it, you take on the "teachings." And when you have finished it, you will have learned something new and fresh and will have the possibility of your own life being forever altered.

—STAN MADSON
Bodhi Tree Bookstore
West Los Angeles

To the Reader

I have been a professional fiction writer for fifty years: seventeen novels published; eight short story collections; twenty theatrical films produced; thirteen television films produced, and more than thirty-five series television scripts produced.

During all of this time, I have read and studied hundreds of books in every branch of metaphysics.

I have used a number of metaphysical ideas in my stories, novels and film and television scripts. But I always felt a need to express them directly and not through fiction.

Thinking and Destiny has made this possible.

In this remarkable work by Harold W. Percival, I believe I have found a book which integrates every conceivable metaphysical concept and answers fully the age-old question: *What is the meaning of life?*

However, because *Thinking and Destiny* is so rich with inspired information, most of which requires extensive study, I have prepared *The Path (A New Look at Reality)* to introduce readers to those concepts in Percival's book which are the easiest to comprehend.

These are taken directly from *Thinking and Destiny*, most of the statements in this book being in Percival's own words.

*　*　*

Why do I characterize *The Path* as *A New Look at Reality*?

Because you may never before have conceived of reality in the manner and/or terms presented in this book.

It is my conviction that basic Reality is not all that perplexing. What seems difficult to assimilate are the manifold *details* of Reality, not its fundamental elements.

This book seeks to address these elements. Elements which mankind must recognize and soon.

Never has there been a period of time more vital to everyone on Earth. It is a period of crucial transition which could well represent mankind's final opportunity to appraise itself and its, (too often), calamitous actions.

Our world is in profound danger. Mankind *must* establish a set of positive values with which to secure its own survival.

This quest for enlightenment must begin *now*.

It is essential that all men and women become aware of what they truly are, why they are here on Earth and what they must do to preserve civilization before it is too late.

I believe that the beginning of this awareness can be found in *The Path*.

RICHARD MATHESON
Los Angeles, California
January 1999

EDITORIAL NOTE

Any editing done by me has been to simplify, never to alter meaning in any way. The use of the words "he," "him," or "man" throughout implies both male and female.

—R. M.

The Path

✤ The First Walk

*W*HEN I WENT FOR A WALK on the day I met the man, my state of mind was dark.

In addition to the problems of my own life, conditions in our country and the world had thoroughly depressed me.

If I had been asked that morning to comment on the meaning of life, my response would have been, "*What* meaning?"

Life, in general, seemed virtually meaningless to me.

✤

There is a path I follow when I walk. Several miles in length, it winds through the community I live in.

I had barely started along the path that morning when I saw a man ahead of me.

He was strolling so leisurely that I overtook him in less than a minute.

As I began to pass him by, he spoke. "Good morning," he said.

I grunted disparagingly. "Not very," I responded.

"Why do you think that?" he asked.

I had no desire for conversation. "Nothing specific," I answered, starting to move away from him.

"May I walk with you?" he asked.

My inclination was to say in a curt, dismissing manner, "*No;* please don't."

But his tone of voice was so disarming that I didn't have the heart to do it.

"I wouldn't be much company," I warned him.

"Not so," he said. "I think you'll be very interesting company indeed."

I had no idea why he would say such a thing, not knowing me at all. But I shrugged and made a submissive sound. "It's up to you," I said.

"*Good*." The man sounded so genuinely pleased that it made me feel guilty for my unfriendly behavior toward him.

He extended his hand as we walked on together. "Delighted to meet you," he said.

That I didn't understand at all. Why should meeting me delight him?

I let it go and, briefly, grasped his hand, looking at him.

He was approximately my height, which is six-foot two, his age somewhere in the middle or late forties, I estimated. He had brown hair and light blue eyes and was wearing an outfit predominantly white—shirt, trousers and jacket. He was a handsome man but it wasn't that which struck me most. It was the expression on his face which took me by surprise.

He seemed the most deeply serene-looking man I had ever met in my life, as though he was possessed of such an inner knowledge and tranquillity that nothing in this world could touch him, much less harm him. I could not help but feel a sense of awe in his presence.

"You live around here?" I asked.

"No." He smiled and shook his head. "This is the first time I've been here."

I presumed that he was staying with someone in the community and said no more. To be truthful, I wasn't interested.

"So," he said. "What is it about the morning that makes it not very good?"

I made a scoffing noise. "What is there that makes it good?" I challenged.

"A beautiful day?" he suggested.

"In a country where one out of every five of our thirty-one million adolescents has at least one serious health problem and can't get basic care?" I said. "In a country where the yearly cost of basic pre-natal care, nutritional guidance and counseling for all prospective mothers can be spent on *one day* of war?"

"You read that article in the morning paper," the man said.

"Yes," I answered, glumly. "I read the newspaper every morning while I'm having coffee. I don't know why I bother. All it does is anger and depress me.

"The article also said that each year half a million children under the age of three go without immunization against the most common childhood diseases. That each year, seventy-five thousand women receive pre-natal care *for the first time* at the moment they enter the delivery room. That the infant mortality rate increases every year."

"It's inexcusable," he said.

"To say the least," I muttered. I blew out aggravated breath. "Schools closing. Teachers underpaid or fired. Mass illiteracy. Child care limited or non-existent. Homeless people mounting in number. Unemployment rising steadily. The wealthy growing wealthier. The poor growing poorer. Drug sales running rampant in the cities. Streets filled with violence. Corruption in politics and business. Military expenditures soaring in the hundreds of billions. Gigantic debts assumed by this generation to be paid off by the next. Stagnant economic growth. The infrastructure collapsing—roads, highways, bridges, airports, sewers, water supply systems. Air and water pollution of every sort. Destruction of the environment. On-going international chaos. Did you say it was a beautiful day?"

We walked in silence for a while before I said, "I'm sorry. I had no right to take that out on you."

"Not at all," he said. "I sympathize. These things are painful to consider."

"You feel as I do then?" I asked.

"Entirely," he said. "These problems could be terminal."

"Is there any answer to them?" I asked. "Or will they just go on until man is extinct?"

"There's always an answer," he replied.

❦

"I'd like to know what it is," I said.

"The people," he told me.

"You mean the voters, don't you?" I asked.

"Primarily, yes," he answered. "Most voters are passive though. They attach themselves to some party, then leave it to their leaders to manage things. They never investigate what's being done. They believe what their leaders say. The voter will likely never make the least effort to know what the man he voted for has actually done in his official capacity."

"I won't argue with that," I told him. "Party politics dominate the country."

"Indeed they do," he said. "In political campaigns, voters become agitated about their party, not about the interests of good government. The most successful party politicians are those who can best reach and control voters through their appetites, weaknesses, selfishness and prejudices."

I looked at him in curiosity. His words seemed fully as provoked as mine. Yet, to my surprise, there was no sign of anger in his voice or expression. How could that be? I was unable to speak of these things without becoming incensed. Yet he seemed perfectly composed.

"Bad government will continue while those who are governed are selfish, indifferent and uninformed," he continued. "So long as people remain blind to the fact that they get what they give individually or as a whole.

"The collective desire of the people will be changed only when people refuse to countenance party politicians who appeal to them for what they know to be wrong.

"Are you saying that we shouldn't have party politics?" I asked.

"Party politics is an enemy to the people because it divides them," he said. "Causes them to be against each other and prevents them from having a united government."

※

I made a sound of quizzical amusement.

"Can't say I see that happening," I said. "The end of party politics? Not likely."

He smiled. "Not for a while at any rate," he agreed.

"You really think," I continued, "that *everyone* is involved in politics only to the extent of his own personal interests?"

"Almost everyone," he said. "Almost everyone adds to the general tendency towards corruption in public institutions."

"Good lord," I said. "Even *I* hadn't thought it was *that* bad." From being totally cynical, I felt somehow defensive now.

"Oh, it's not that there are no men at all who would be good officials," he said. "The problem is that the people don't appreciate or uphold such officials. They forsake them and leave them disappointed. Force them to protect themselves by complaisance or by corruption."

"Is it all hopeless then?" I asked. Odd how my position had been altered from outrage to appeal by the finality of his words.

He smiled at the sound in my voice and doubtless the look on my face.

"Not at all," he said. "While it's true that the majority of people are uninformed, their thoughts largely superficial or callous, there are, among humanity, many who have fundamental virtues; whose thoughts have made them honest, self-respecting, even self-sacrificing. Usually, such people play no public role, however, for the public wouldn't have them. But they help to restore the balance."

"What about the public?" I asked. "Don't they ever change for the better?" Curious how I quickly accepted his words as truth.

"When the thoughts of the people demand a change for the better, someone usually appears to fight for it," he said. "That someone acts because of being impelled to act and allowed to see the way to accomplish the needed purpose. These are generally unconscious agents of the people. Group-will calls for an instrument by which the people's desires can be realized, and that instrument appears."

❦

"You know," the man went on, "we must always keep one thing in mind. The present stage in social development is not more than a halfway toward civilization. It's still theoretical and outward, not yet practical and inward. This is shown by the prisons, the law courts, the police forces in towns and cities to prevent or hold in check murder, robbery, rape and general disorder."

I knew my smile to be grim. "Not to mention war," I added.

"Of course," he said. "The world's half-formed civilization is even more glaringly demonstrated by the ways in which governments have turned invention, science and industry into the manufacture of ammunitions and machines of death for the conquest of other lands. While wars exist, the world cannot be civilized."

"And yet what has war ever truly accomplished?" I said more than asked.

"Very little," he responded. "History stretches from the present into the dim and forgotten past as a fading record of the achievements of the conquered and their conquerors who were, in their own turn, conquered. The law of might has been the law of life and death by which civilizations of the past have risen and fallen."

I wondered again how he could speak of such things with such equanimity in his voice. Was he that far above it? The concept perplexed me.

"Murder and savagery have been the practice of the nations of the earth," he continued. "The blessings and benefits of centuries of agriculture and manufacturing, of research, literature, invention, science and discovery and the accumulation of wealth is still being used by nations for the murder and destruction of each other."

"*Why*?" I asked; I think I sounded almost plaintive. "Why does it go on and on?"

"Because the basic human problem goes on and on," he replied.

"Which is what?" I asked.

"Which is: *Shall reason rule the body or shall the body control reason*?" he said.

"When the body is the master and reason is made to serve the base impulses of the body, then the people are in essence, brutes. Individuals war among themselves and people war against other people, morals and laws ignored or forgotten."

"It *is* that bad, isn't it?" I said disconsolately.

"It is indeed," he said; clearly, he had not yet completed his grim assessment of mankind's shortcomings.

"Though they are of one family, human beings have hunted each other with more ferocity and cruelty than beasts of the jungle," he continued. "Predacious animals hunt only for food. But men hunt to rob others of their possessions and to enslave them. Human law has been made by might and the law of might has been accepted as the law of right."

"Dear God," I murmured. "I know it's true but..." I couldn't finish the remark. I sighed heavily. "Is there no answer then?" I asked.

"There is always an answer," he replied.

"What *is* it then?" I asked, feeling as gloomy as I ever had in my life.

"War made by one people on another must be recognized as national murder and the people who provoke that war condemned as murderers. Grievances of any kind must be settled by negotiations or arbitrations under judges agreed upon."

"Is there no such thing as a *just* war then?" I asked.

"The only just war is in defense of democracy," he said. "A war for conquest, for business or for plunder is *against* democracy and should be opposed by the people."

"*Our* democracy?" I asked

"*Everyone's*," he responded. "For the safety of world civilization, there should be a democracy of nations."

"How do we manage that?" I asked.

"By example," he answered. "The United States should be the nation among nations to establish a real democracy so that the excellence of its government will be so apparent that the other nations will adopt democracy as the best form of government."

"What prevents that?" I asked.

"You tell me," he said.

I had to smile, albeit gravely. "What are you, a teacher or something?" I asked.

"You might say that," he replied. "But tell me. What do you think prevents the United States from becoming a real democracy?"

I thought about it for several moments as we walked. Finally, I suggested, "Greed?"

"That certainly is part of it," he said. "A big part. The quest for money."

Ah, yes, money, I thought. I was scarcely immune from that quest myself.

"The problem is," he said, "that after money was established as the medium of exchange, people centered their interest in *it* instead of in the things for which it was exchanged."

"Which did what?" I asked.

"Created money mania," he answered.

I had to chuckle. "*Money mania*?"

He nodded but didn't smile. "The race for money has made man a money maniac," he said. "Ever before him is one leading thought represented by gain and profit. After one is infected by the contagion of money mania, he cannot analyze his condition."

"Is it all that simple?" I asked.

"Too often it is," he said. "Though behind the concept of business, there should be other purposes than making money."

"Such as?" I asked.

"*Character* should be the true basis and strength of business," he said. "Business can never be sound and trustworthy if it's based only on the accumulation of money. Since business transactions depend largely on credit, that credit must depend on character, not money.

"Eventually, there should be an institution such as a Money Department in the government. With such a department, there would be confidence in business and money would be put in its proper place.

"Now, instead of understanding that it's responsible for the strength of the government, big business strives instead to acquire special advantages from the government."

"I've always thought that was monstrous," I said.

"Of course it is," he agreed. "It's monstrous for big business to control government. And the cancerous disease of big business continues to spread. As it grows beyond the need of its community, it spreads to other cities and states in the nation, then to other nations until it spreads to all the nations of the world.

"Then the big business of each nation struggles with the big business of other nations. And the big business of each nation demands that its government protect its interest. There are exchanges of complaints and threats of governments and possible war.

"Ever-expanding big business is one of the major troubles of the people of the world," he finished.

"There's another side to this, though," I said.

"Which is?" he asked.

"To play the devil's advocate," I said. "Isn't just as much trouble caused by labor as by management?"

"Certainly capital cannot do without labor any more than labor can do without capital," he concluded. "The problem is, of course, that the two have not yet learned to work together for their own common good.

"When capital and labor really understand the facts by putting itself in the other's place, they won't continue to delude themselves. Instead of being enemies, they will, from necessity, become co-workers for the common good."

"How does money fit into all this?" I asked.

"Money cannot be considered to be capital," he answered. "Brain and brawn and time are capital. Money is only the resultant product. A product which should be divided by capital and labor in due proportion to their vested interests."

"Sounds like pie in the sky to me," I said. "How can that ever come to be?"

"If the people demand it," he said.

※

"The people again," I said.

"It's always the people," he responded.

"When the demand of the people is strong enough, business must comply because there can be no business without the people. Business—*and* government, of course—are the representatives of the people. The question is, do the people really *want* honest government and honest business?"

"*Don't* they?" I asked, surprised.

"If they do, then they themselves must be honest," he said. "It stands to reason that, from self-interest alone, the people can have honest government and honest business only by being honest themselves.

"Then and only then will they have a real democracy."

"You've used that phrase a number of times now," I remarked. "I take it you're implying that the United States doesn't have a real democracy."

"Do you think it does?" he countered.

"Well, we *should*," I responded. "If *we* don't have it, who on earth does?"

"Of course," he said. "Of all the surface of the earth, the new lands of America offered the fairest opportunity for the birth of a new people in an atmosphere of freedom, under a new government.

"But this freedom was from the restraints that had been put on them in the countries from which they came. It was not freedom from their own greed and brutalities. People believe, you see, that they are free because they are not slaves or not imprisoned. But they are just as imprisoned by the desires of their senses.

"In addition, too many people believe that liberty gives them the right to say and do what they please regardless of the rights of others. *This is simply not true*. Liberty is a social state in which one respects and gives the same consideration to the rights of others as he expects for his own."

"I have often found," I said, "that people who insist the most vehemently on equal rights usually want more than their rights."

"Usually," the man agreed. "But true equality in freedom is that *each person* has the right to think, to feel, to do as he wills without force, pressure or restraint. One cannot usurp the rights of another without invalidating his own rights."

"Can't the government enforce this?" I asked.

"Not really," he answered. "The government can make no man free, law-abiding and just any more than it can determine his destiny and give him happiness. The laws of the country guarantee a citizen liberty in his *pursuit* of happiness. But the laws cannot *provide* that happiness. Man himself must determine what his life will be."

The man stopped abruptly and looked at me.

"Remember this," he said. "No limits can be set to man's rise to heights of the sublime. Yet no beast can sink to the depths of the depravities of man.

"He is kind and compassionate. He is also cruel and merciless. He is loving and considerate of others. Yet he hates and is rapacious. He'll devote his energies to revealing the ills and troubles of others. Yet no theological devil can compare with the fiendishness of man."

"Why does that never change?" I asked.

"Because man will not make known to himself the enigma he is," he said. "It's easier to pull down mountains and build up cities. These things he can see and handle. But he can't find the way to his true self."

"What is his true self?" I asked.

He smiled. "We'll speak of that another time," he said. "We've talked enough today."

He startled me by walking off without another word.

I watched for several moments before calling after him.

"We haven't introduced each other."

"Another time," he said.

It was the end of my first walk with the man.

🌿 Second Walk

I AVOIDED WALKING for the next few days. I thought I might accost the man and I didn't want that. His refusal to introduce himself had irritated me. What reason could he have for doing that? It seemed somehow offensive to me. So I didn't walk for two days, then three.

On the fourth, however, I realized that I wanted to see him again, to talk with him. Did it really make any difference if he introduced himself or not? It was not his name I was interested in but what he had to say.

So, on the fourth day, after I had read the morning newspaper and had my coffee, I went for a walk along the path.

I had been on it for a short while when, turning a bend, I saw him walking up ahead.

For an instant, I had an impulse to turn and go back before he saw me. I realized, at that moment, that it wasn't irritation because he hadn't introduced himself.

It was uneasiness about what he might tell me this time.

Somehow, I sensed that I was at a mental crossroad. If I continued on, I might be unable to go back. Ideas presented to me might remain fixed in my consciousness and, conceivably, change my life.

Did I really want that?

Information, yes. Enlightenment. But challenge? An irreversible summons to advance my awareness?

Was I ready for it?

🌿

Perhaps the man sensed what I was thinking for he solved the problem by stopping and looking around with a smile.

"Good morning," he said, pleasantly. "I'm happy to see you again."

"Good morning," I replied. I could not retreat now. Whatever lay ahead, I was committed to it.

He waited until I'd joined him, then we walked on together.

"Have you thought of what we talked about on our walk together?" was the first thing he asked.

It came to me instantly. "I've been thinking about little else," I confessed. "I can't get any work done. I just keep thinking."

"*Good*." He sounded pleased to hear that. "Thinking is important. *All* important."

"I suppose it is," I admitted.

"So," he said, "what would you like to talk about today?"

I smiled. "Real democracy?" I suggested.

"Why not?" he agreed. "Real democracy. Which is to say, of course, democracy as *self-government*."

"The people?" I asked.

He nodded. "Democracy as self-government is what people of all nations are blindly seeking," he said. "No matter how different or opposed their forms or methods seem to be, real democracy is what all people inherently want because it will allow them the most freedom with the greatest opportunity and security."

"Has it ever been achieved?" I asked. Strange how quickly, I had re-assumed a student-teacher attitude.

"There have been numerous attempts at democracies," he said. "But there has never been a real democracy among human beings because, instead of honest thought and freedom of speech, the people have always allowed themselves to be flattered and deceived, bought and sold.

"To have a real democracy, the voters who elect representatives from among themselves to govern *must themselves be self-governed*."

"And if they managed to achieve this?" I asked.

"Then voters would know enough to select and elect representatives who are qualified to govern in the interests of all the people."

"But now they don't," I said.

"But now they don't," he repeated. "Now their self-interest renders them easy victims to impostors.

"Astute and power-loving pretenders beguile the people by promising what they cannot or would not give. They shake their heads and fists and make the air tremble with their 'sympathies' for the poor, long-suffering and abused people. They paint alluring word-pictures and describe what they'll do for the people to deliver them from the misery and bondage they're in.

"If they were to say what they actually intended to do, they'd have to say, 'When I have authority over you, my will shall be your law and I'll compel you to do what I say and be what I want you to be'."

"You make it sound like some kind of cynical game," I told him.

"Democracy as it's practiced is a game," he said. "A game between the 'ins' and the 'outs.' The players vie for offices for personal and party power and plunder. That can hardly be called real democracy."

※

"Still, always keep in mind," he added, "the success or failure of democracy doesn't depend on dishonest politicians.

"Politicians are only what people make them or allow them to be. *The success or failure of democracy depends primarily on the people*. This cannot be emphasized enough.

"No power on earth can make a real democracy for the people. If the people are to have a real democracy, the government must be *made* a real democracy by the people themselves."

"The ballot is a precious thing then," I said.

"*Absolutely*," he agreed; I had never heard his tone so passionate. "It is a symbol of what could be the highest civilization of man. A symbol to be valued above birth or possessions—above rank or party or class.

"The symbol by which each one of the people is pledged to use the right and power vested in him to preserve, under law and justice, equal rights and freedom for all."

"A symbol constantly misused," I added.

"Constantly," he agreed. "Instead of each of the citizens looking to the interests of all the people, the greater number of citizens have neglected the public welfare. Taken whatever personal advantages they could get for themselves and allowed the government to be taken over by political tricksters."

"The game again?" I asked.

He nodded gravely. "The game," he said. "Foxes and wolves contesting for the citizen-sheep who vote them into power. Playing the citizen-sheep against each other in the game of special interests: 'Capital' versus 'Labor,' 'Labor' versus 'Capital.' A game to see which side can succeed in giving up the least and getting the most."

"With the voter losing the game?" I suggested.

"Invariably," he said. "As long as the people tolerate the claim of the incoming party that 'to the victors belong the spoils,' so long will the people themselves continue to *be* the spoils."

"Still, the people keep looking for leaders," I said.

"Always," he said. "Yet no one man or group of men can save the country. Men who are great and imbued with the responsibility of leadership are certainly to be desired. But the obvious fact is that however great a few men may be as champions of the peoples' rights, they cannot succeed unless the people are determined to do what's necessary to maintain a real democracy.

"That is the issue which the public refuses to face," he continued. "That blame and responsibility in a democracy should be charged mainly to the people.

"Yet if the people will not select and elect the best and most able men to govern, then they must suffer the consequences of their own indifference, their own prejudices, their own collusion and connivance at wrong-doing."

He shook his head slowly.

"And the pity of it all," he said, "is that the foundation for a real democracy was carefully formulated when the United States came into being."

"What was that?" I asked.

"The Constitution," he said.

❦

"Oh. Yes." I nodded awkwardly. "Of course. One tends to forget about it."

"That's a pity too," he said, "because it is the greatest blessing ever bestowed on a people who desire freedom. The Constitution puts the supreme power of government in the hands of the people.

"It gives to each citizen a clear right to be, to will, to do or to have anything which he or she is able to be, to will, to do or to have.

"But if the people are not vitally interested in having and in holding the power of self-government, that power will be taken from them. Then, instead of the government being dependent on the people, the people are dependent on the government."

"I think that's easier said than done," I broke in. "With the advanced state of the media, it's so easy to delude the people nowadays."

"Granted," he said. "Which makes it all the more important that the public remain alert and informed. Not victimized by party politics."

"The Constitution didn't condone party politics, did it?" I asked.

"Not at all," he said. "According to the Constitution, power is not to be with any party or person. *The people are to have the power.*"

"It didn't exactly work out that way, did it?" I said.

"Unfortunately, no." He shook his head. "And in party government, the good of the party comes first. Then, perhaps, the good of the country. Last, the good of the people.

"The people cannot get men who will protect their interests because those whom the people elect are selected by their parties and pledged to their parties.

"The people cannot have a real democracy as long as the game of party politics continues."

"Whose blame *is* this?" I asked.

"The *people*, " he said. "*The people are the ones who are responsible.* They don't wish to govern themselves. They prefer others to run the government for them.

"Accordingly, they don't take the trouble to look into the character of the politicians they elect. They are easily deceived because their own cupidity encourages them to be beguiled. So the politicians play the game. And the people *are* the game."

"Are all party politicians dishonest then?" I asked.

"No, no, not all," he said. "They're not all wicked and un-scrupulous. They're merely human and their human nature urges them to use trickery to win the people. The people have, in fact, *taught* them that if they don't use trickery, they'll almost surely lose the game. Many of those who've lost the game know this, so they play to win now."

"What exactly should the people do?" I asked.

"Instead of continuing to teach the politicians how to win them over by deceiving them, the people should teach those who aspire to government office that they will no longer suf-fer themselves to be the game and the spoils.

"The people *themselves* should nominate from the notable men before the public those whom they consider to be the worthiest in character and the best qualified to fill the offices for which they're nominated. And from the nominees, the people should elect the ones they believe to be the best quali-fied to govern."

"I doubt if party politicians would like that very much," I said, unable to suppress amusement.

"Of *course* they wouldn't like it," he said. "They'd hate it because they'd lose their jobs as party politicians. They'd lose control of the people and break up their own game. They'd lose their share of the profits from grants and contracts, from court and other appointments.

"They'd lose their ability to separate the people into as many divisions as there are parties. Lose their ability to make their own platforms and contrive their own policies to attract and capture the people who might become their partisans."

"Can this really be made to work?" I asked, doubting it.

"Of course it can," he said firmly. "If the people refuse to be hoodwinked by parties and party politicians. If the people demand that government posts be given only to those who are independent and responsible, such candidates will be forthcoming."

※

"You know," he said, "when people look back from the future—when they see things and conditions more truly as they are—the politics of today will seem incredible to them.

"They'll see that party politicians acted more like those wolves and foxes I mentioned before than they did like normal human beings. That each political party used every conceivable means to discredit the others and get the favor of the people in order to get possession of the government."

"How *far* into the future?" I asked.

"That depends entirely on the people," he answered. "They must realize that they're responsible for all that they think and all that they do. That it isn't right for them to depend on anyone or to let others do for them what they can do and *should* do for themselves.

"The truth of the matter," he continued, "is that the world does not need to be made safe for democracy. It is the *people* who must be safe for democracy—and for the world. They cannot have a real democracy until each one of them begins his self-government at home.

"When man is shown that he helps to make the laws by which he lives and is governed—when he understands that his destiny in life is made by his own thoughts and acts—then it will be self-evident to him that he cannot do to another what he would not want others to do to him."

"The golden rule," I said.

He smiled and nodded. "The golden rule."

I thought about what he'd said for several moments, then asked, "How much longer does man have to *reach* this level of understanding?"

"The brutality in man in seeking for himself only so he can survive by his might over others has gone about as far as it can," he said.

"The old way has been: the one or the few against the many or the many against the one or the few.

"The new way is: The one or the few *for* the many and the many for each one and for all.

"This is the right way of life to real democracy.

"What is against the interest of any individual is to the disadvantage of all the people.

"This fundamental fact about democracy has never been dealt with.

"Because of that, democracy has always failed in every past civilization in its time of trail.

"It is now again on trial.

"The people are now determining the kind of democracy they will have in the future. Shall they continue in the devious way of make-believe democracy? Or shall they take the straight way to real democracy?

"There is danger in delay. This is the time to settle the question.

"Will the people have a democracy in name only or will they become a real democracy?

"The steps cannot be taken by only a few of the people. And to date the greater number have not shown that they understand or have thought at all about what a real democracy is.

"The people must become conscious that they need fear no one more than themselves. They are responsible for civilization. And if civilization is to continue, the people must become self-responsible.

"There is no other way."

※

"Civilization is not only for ourselves," he continued. "Not only for our children's children.

"Civilization is for *permanence*—to continue through all flowing time.

"The fundamentals of American democracy are excellent but the preferences and prejudices and ungoverned weaknesses of the people prevent the practice of those fundamentals.

"Only a few are to be blamed for the mistakes of the past.

"But all should be blamed if they continue the mistakes.

"Now is the time for bringing into existence a *real democracy*. One that will continue through the ages because it will be based on the principles of truth, of rightness and reason, law and justice.

"At this crucial period of civilization, new and terrible powers have been revealed. If used solely for destructive purposes, they could sound the parting knell for life on earth as we know it.

"Now is the time to stem the approaching avalanche. There is a duty for each individual to perform: *to govern himself.*

"Democracy *can* be made the permanent government of mankind. The people must not let this opportunity be destroyed. Democracy *can* be a government for all the people by the will of the people, in the interest of all the people.

"Then each of them will have the opportunity for achievement and progress. The opportunity to achieve what is desired and to be what each one wills to be. To constantly progress in capacity. To become conscious of what one truly is."

"Which is *what*" I asked. "You said something like that on our first walk but I don't know what you mean."

"Next time," he said, starting away from me.

I stopped in my tracks. You're doing it *again*? I thought, incredulous. I'm *still* not going to know who you are?

I stood speechless as I watched him move off.

It was the end of our second walk together.

✾ Third Walk

ONCE AGAIN, I avoided walking for the next few days.

I realized fully now, however, that it wasn't irritation at the man's apparent unwillingness to identify himself.

I really was uneasy about what seemed to be happening to me.

I had the definite feeling that I'd suggested talking about real democracy on our second walk not because the subject was all *that* fascinating to me. We had, in fact, discussed similar points during our first walk.

It was, instead, as though I was avoiding the subject he had broached at the end of both walks.

The true self.

Did I really want to talk about that, learn about that?

Something about the subject made me uncomfortable.

It was, I sensed, a subject that might move too close to me. Threaten to draw me into areas of thought I'd avoided, before.

Politics and government I could assimilate and deal with.

But the true self?

My true self?

To be honest, the concept alarmed me.

✾

Still, as before, I could not maintain my resolve to avoid walking again. Meeting the man again and talking with him. Listening, really; I'd done very little speaking as I recalled. It *was* as though he was the teacher and I was his student.

The problem was that I didn't know what course he was teaching and whether I was prepared to take it, much less earn a passing grade.

Nonetheless, again on the fourth day, after my morning coffee and my reading the newspaper, I left the house and walked to the path. I had no doubt that I would meet the man again. I almost felt that he'd been waiting for me every day since our last walk together.

I will never know if that is literally true.

I only know that I had barely started along the path when I saw him up ahead.

This time, he wasn't walking. He was standing in the sunlight, waiting for me. And, suddenly, it was as though we both knew that I had no choice in the matter.

I *had* to walk with him again and learn whatever he elected to teach me.

"Good morning," I said, the first to speak.

He nodded, smiling, clearly pleased to see me. "Good morning to you," he replied.

I hesitated for a few moments, then inquired, "Have you been waiting for me?"

"Yes, I have," he admitted.

"For the last four days?"

He smiled. "I knew you'd come," he said.

I sighed, feeling a sense of almost helplessness. Was I that transparent to him?

I decided to regain some sense of presence by extending my hand abruptly and telling him my name.

I looked at him expectantly, waiting for his reply.

"You want me to introduce myself," he said.

I waited.

"It's difficult for me to do that," he told me.

I felt a faint twinge of satisfaction that I had, at least momentarily, put him on the defensive. I continued to wait.

He smiled then. "Think of me as your companion," he said.

I frowned. "No name?"

"No name."

"*Why?*" I demanded. "Is your identity that mysterious?"

"No," he said. "Someday, I'll tell you. Though a name will always be a problem. But please, for now. Your companion?"

I exhaled slowly. I wasn't sure if I was willing to accept this condition from him. I could balk if I wanted to, turn and move away from him in aggravation.

I knew then that such a thing was impossible.

I couldn't leave.

I had to keep walking with him.

Learning from him.

"Very well," I said. "If that's the way it has to be," I grunted. "My companion then," I said.

"*Good*." He smiled. "And, believe me, I'm not doing this for the sake of being mysterious. Someday, I'll explain.

"All right," I submitted.

He patted me gently on the back. "Shall we continue along the path then?" he asked.

I nodded. "Fine."

We started off.

※

"You know," I said, "I thought our last walk was a little short."

"It was," he agreed.

"Any reason for that?" I asked.

"Yes," he said. "When I asked you what you'd like to talk about, you suggested 'real democracy'."

"And...?" I didn't understand what he was getting at.

"For our purpose," he told me, "there wasn't that much more to say about it. So the walk was short."

I looked at him, guardedly now.

Our *purpose*?

What did *that* mean?

I asked.

"Well, you see," he said, "we're heading in a specific direction."

"On the path you mean?" I misunderstood.

"The path of ideas," he said.

I thought about that for several moments as we walked.

"Let me guess," I said then. "The last thing you said on our last walk was that the purpose of real democracy was to help us become conscious of what we truly are."

"Correct." He nodded.

"And at the end of our first walk, you spoke about man's true self."

"Correct again," he said, smiling at me.

"Then I guess that's what we're due to talk about now," I said.

"Only if you wish it," he assured me.

I swallowed, feeling uneasy again. *Did* I wish it?

I thought about it for what seemed to be a long while as we walked in silence.

Finally, I realized that I felt compelled to learn about this true self whatever it might be.

"I wish it," I told him.

"Good." He smiled. "Then let's begin."

"To understand what you truly are," he began, "you must first see clearly the distinction between yourself and the body you live in."

Oh boy, here we go, I thought.

"You should know that you are not your body. You should know that your body is not you.

"The body you are in is not you any more than your body is the clothes that your body wears.

"Take your body out of the clothes it wears and the clothes fall down. They cannot move without the body.

"Similarly, when the 'you' in your body leaves your body, your body falls down and sleeps or is dead. Your body is unconscious. There is no feeling, no desire, no thinking in your body. Your body cannot do anything of itself without the conscious 'you'."

"Oh, boy," I murmured.

"What?" He smiled at the sound in my voice.

"From party politics to this," I said

"The progression is inevitable," he replied.

I nodded, bracing myself. "Okay," I said. "Go on."

"You're sure." He looked at me in concern.

I swallowed. "No, I'm not," I said. "But I want to go on anyway."

"All right." He nodded. "Your reflection on this simple truth compels you to realize that you definitely are not and cannot be your body. Rather your body is a physical organism. That you live in a living nature mechanism that you are operating. An animal that you are trying to understand, to train, to master."

He smiled at my expression. "Are you with me so far?" he asked.

"With you." I nodded. I wasn't certain if I really was but I was determined to continue as though I was.

"Very well," he said. "Next point. You know the name by which your body is distinguished from the bodies of others. And this you have learned to think of as *your* name, *your* identity."

Did this have anything to do with his claim that he couldn't give himself a name? I wondered.

Who knew? My head was already spinning. *Stay with it*, I ordered myself.

❦

"Your body had a beginning and it will have an end," the man continued. "And from beginning to end it is subject to the laws of the world phenomena, of change and of time.

"Your body and its senses have no power of voluntary functioning; no more than your glove through which you are able to feel and act. Rather, that power is in you, the operator. The conscious self."

He raised his right arm, gesturing around us.

"You know about the atmosphere of Earth," he said.

"Yes." I regarded him closely, thinking, what now?

"Well," he continued, "just as there is an atmosphere of the Earth in which, you might say, the Earth breathes and lives, maintains its form and has its being—so, too, is there an atmosphere into which, as an infant, man is born and maintains *his* being."

"This atmosphere is the first thing man takes on and it is the last thing that, as a physical being, he gives up.

"This atmosphere is not an indefinite and uncertain quantity. It has a definite outline and qualities. It may be perceptible to the senses and is known to the mind.

"If one could see the physical atmosphere of a man, it would appear as innumerable particles in a room, made visible by a ray of sunlight.

"These would be seen to be circling or whirling about the body, all kept in movement by his breath.

"They would be seen to reach out, circle about and return into his body, following it wherever it goes and affecting the particles of other physical atmospheres with which it comes into contact."

"Ah-*ha*," I mumbled.

He looked at me dryly. "Yes?" he asked.

"A bit of a far cry from the ballot box." I said.

He laughed. "Indeed." He paused. "You want to stop?" he asked.

The sound I made was one of weak surrender. As though I *could* stop now, I thought. "Forge on." I said, part of me amused, part dazed.

"All right," he said. "Continuing then.

"Man's lifelong search for 'something' to satisfy his inner self is, in reality, the quest for this true self. This identity which each one of us is dimly conscious of and *feels* and desires to know.

"This conscious self in the body has been called many things but, for our purpose, we'll call it the *doer-in-the-body*."

Our *purpose* again, I thought. What did that *mean?*

"Think of yourself," he said, "as an embodied doer."

"What *is* this 'doer'?" I asked. "Male? Female?"

"The doer has no sex," he answered. "It is neither male nor female. It possesses, in fact, the characteristic nature of both."

"How does that work?" I asked.

"If the doer expresses itself as a male, it shows the nature of a man and does the things that men do; the body is masculine. The female side is suppressed."

"And if the body is female?" I asked.

"The male side of the doer is suppressed," he answered. "The doer expresses itself as a female. It shows the nature of a woman and does the things that women do."

"Is this...*doer* aware of all this?" I asked.

He shook his head. "The doer doesn't know who or what it is. Although it may mistakenly suppose that it is, in fact, the body which it inhabits approximately sixteen of the twenty-four hours a day."

"What *is* it exactly?" I asked.

"Your true self," he said. "Immortal. Changeless. Forever beyond the reach of the phenomena of change and time. Of death."

"Whoa, whoa," I said. "This true self continues *after death*?" I felt my pulse beat racing at the thought.

"Let's talk about sleep first," he said.

❦

"*Sleep*?" I looked at him in curiosity.

He nodded. "Do you ever wonder why you sleep?"

I thought about it for a short while before I had to admit, "Rarely."

"Consider," he told me, "our bodies are unconscious for approximately a third of our life span. Now either something very valuable is going on or we're wasting a lot of time, wouldn't you say?"

The question made me chuckle. "I suppose we sleep in order to rest," I said.

"Is that what science tells us?" he asked.

I thought about that. "I don't know what science tells us," I had to confess. "All I've ever read about is what happens to us if we *don't* sleep."

"Sleep deprivation," he said.

I nodded. "They seem to have much information about that."

"But not on *why* we sleep," he said.

"All right," I responded. "Why *do* we sleep?"

"In order that nature may be allowed to re-condition your body without the interference of your thoughts and emotions," he said, "it is provided that you periodically let go of it.

"Nature in your body provides that the bond which holds you and the senses is, at times, relaxed—partially or completely.

"This relaxation—or letting go of the senses—is sleep.

"Going to sleep is the withdrawal of the doer from directing the body. In sleep, there is no conscious feeling because the doer has withdrawn from contact with the body."

"Aren't there different kinds of sleep?" I asked.

"Two," he said. "Sleep is either deep or dream.

"Deep sleep is the state in which you withdraw completely into yourself; in which you are totally out of touch with the senses.

"It is the state in which the senses have stopped functioning as the result of having been disconnected from the power by which they function. Which power is you. The doer.

"Dream sleep on the other hand is a state of *partial* detachment. A state in which your senses are turned from the outer objects of nature to function *inwardly* in nature."

"When does dream sleep take place?" I asked.

"When the doer is withdrawing from the senses into the state of deep sleep. And during the time when the doer is *returning* from deep sleep to its connection with the senses."

"How long do we remain in deep sleep?" I asked.

"That depends on the length of time the physical body needs in which to be repaired and refreshed," he said.

"And this can only be done if this doer as you call it withdraws entirely from the body?" I asked.

"That's correct," he said. "During sleep, forces are at work to repair the damage sustained by the body during working hours while it is driven by the double commands of nature and the doer.

"The forces can only make these repairs when there is no interference by the doer. Then electrical currents can stimulate and magnetic waves bathe the atoms, molecules, cells, organs and systems. Waste is removed. Body parts are properly related to each other and the systems keyed up."

Sounds like quite a process, I thought. "And when this is finished?" I asked.

"As soon as the repairs to the physical structure are made," he answered, "the doer re-enters its stations in the body, returns to the waking state and—suddenly or gradually— becomes conscious of its feeling in the physical world.

"You awaken the senses and begin to function through them again as the intelligent operator of your machine. And, from life-long habit, you identify yourself as your body.

"'I have been asleep,' you say. 'Now I am awake.'"

"But *the body isn't you*," I said, trying to get it fixed in my mind.

"*The body isn't you*," he repeated. "Although your body changes the material of which it is composed oftener than you change your clothes, your identity does not change. You are always the same you.

"In your body or out of it. Awake or asleep, day after day. Through life and through death and all states after death. From life to life through all your lives, your identity —"

"*Whoa!*" I cried. "Through *all our lives*? You're talking about *reincarnation* now?"

"We'll get to that," he said, smiling. "For now, just keep in mind that this self, this *you*, which is conscious throughout your present life, is the *same* self, the *same* you, that was conscious of continuing day after day through each of your former lives."

I started to object, then fell back mentally. Okay, I thought. He said we'll get to it. Take his word for it. Just *listen*.

Which I did—albeit somewhat benumbed.

"Remember this," the man told me. "A day and a lifetime are essentially the same. Both are recurring periods of a continuous existence.

"Sleep and death are very much alike. When you slip away to let your body rest, you go through an experience very similar to that which you go through when you leave the body at death.

"*Death is no more than a prolonged sleep.*

"*A temporary retirement from the human world.*

"The long sleep of death will not affect the continuity of your identity any more than your nightly sleep affects it.

"What is more, your nightly dreams may be compared to the after-death states through which you regularly pass.

"*Both are phases of purely subjective activity in the doer.*

"And the nightly period of deep sleep, when the senses no longer function, corresponds to that blank period in which your soul waits on the threshold of the physical world until the moment you re-connect —"

"*Hold* it," I said, raising my right hand like a traffic cop.

He stopped and looked at me questioningly.

"I'm sorry," I said, "but this is going too fast for me.

"For two walks, we discuss party politics and government and real democracy. Now suddenly, we're into embodied doers and life-after-death and reincarnation and souls. *I just can't keep up with you.*"

He smiled and stopped walking, gripping me by the arms.

I cannot describe the feeling it gave me, as though an immeasurable force was coursing through me.

I wavered slightly as he let go of me.

"We'll go more slowly," he promised.

I blinked and shook my head to clear it. "I'd appreciate that," I murmured.

"Only one more thing to remember now," he said, smiling.

"*The soul is an actual and living fact.* For our purpose, we'll call it the *breath-form*. The senior, presiding unit in the body.

"Every human being that comes into this world is fashioned by its mother according to this form—the soul—which enters the body through her breath and —"

He broke off, smiling at my expression. "Later," he said. "Just keep in mind that, when the doer separates from the body at death, the breath-form, the soul, leaves with it."

"What *happens* when we die?" I asked.

"We'll talk about that on our next walk, shall we?" he said.

I stood in silence while he moved away from me. *Where does he go when he leaves me?* I wondered.

It was the end of our third walk.

🌿 Fourth Walk

I DIDN'T HESITATE this time. No point in looking for excuses. I was hooked. I wanted to know more.

And more.

The only questions in my mind as I left my house the next morning—having had only my coffee, ignoring the newspaper—were who this man was and how it was that I had come to meet him.

Had it been an accident? A happy accident, that is.

I was astonished by the trust I had in him. Astonished by my total willingness to accept a student-teacher relationship with him.

I had no way of proving whether what he'd told me was true or not.

All I knew was that I doubted not a syllable of it.

For me, that was incredible.

I had always been—at least for many years had been— the sort who demanded proof for everything.

Now here I was accepting one man's words regarding the most far-reaching, demanding of subjects.

Why?

And where were these walks and conversations leading me?

That question was the most daunting of all.

🌿

He was waiting for me at the foot of the path.

"You didn't wait four days this time," he said, smiling.

"I won't be doing that again," I told him.

He patted me on the back. "Good," he said. "We have much to talk about."

I felt a thrill of prescience at this words.

I was ready to hear whatever he had to tell me.

"Shall we?" he said, gesturing toward the path.

I nodded and we began to walk.

"All right," I said, immediately. "Life after death. How does it work?"

It impressed me that, not for a moment, was I questioning the existence of life after death. Only the way in which it functioned.

Remarkable, I thought, looking to him for the answer to my question.

⚘

"First of all," he began, "let me explain the four physical units which constitute the human body. These are the solid body—which we know—and what we call the *fluid* body, the *airy* body and the *radiant* body, which is also called the *astral* body.

"Emanations from these bodies extend as zones around the solid body. Together they make up the physical atmosphere of the human body."

"Is that the breath-form you mentioned?" I asked.

"No, the breath-form is different," he answered. "Made up of much finer matter which *shapes* the form of the astral body."

"I think I've got it," I said, not sure that I did.

"For now, just keep in mind the astral body," he told me.

"Dying is the withdrawal of that body from the physical body.

"As it recedes, rigor mortis sets in. The regions left become cold and there is no feeling in them. Then the three bodies hover or flutter over the heart and puff themselves out of the mouth with the last breath, causing a slight gurgle in the throat."

"Is that what they refer to as the death rattle?" I asked.

"Exactly," he said, nodding.

"What about the breath-form?" I asked. "The *doer*. What happens to them when you die?"

"They hover over the physical body like a cloud," he said. "Or they may stand in human form beside or above the body.

"If death has not yet taken place, there is a slight cord that connects these finer bodies with the heart or some other part of the physical body."

"Is that what they call the silver cord?" I asked.

"It's been called that, yes," he responded.

"There is no actual death until this connection is broken. It is broken when the breath-form leaves. This happens when the doer desires, consents or wills to die.

"The doer is attached to life, however, and, at first, refuses to die. But when it knows that it is useless to cling to the body, it wills to die and death is instantaneous."

※

"This is probably off the subject," I said, "but which is it better to do, bury the body or cremate it?"

"Not off the subject at all," he said. "It's extremely important to the subject.

"Cremation is the best disposition of the body after death. By burning, the material of the body is restored to the elements from which it came."

"And burial?" I asked.

"Embalming and burial are bad," he answered. "These methods hold the three bodies with the flesh for a long time—until the flesh body has decayed.

"In this way, the physical atmosphere of the body is not destroyed and it's possible for the doer with its breath-form to go back to its old 'haunts'."

"You mean become a ghost?" I asked.

"It's possible," he said.

"So the sooner the body is disposed of, the better."

"The more quickly it's disposed of, the better it is for the entities composing it," he replied. "For the doer. And, for that matter, for the people of the world."

His unexpected last words made me shudder at the images it fostered in my mind.

"What about the astral body?" I asked to change the subject. "Does it 'move on' or what?"

"No, no," he said. "After death, the astral body loses touch with the breath-form and is as dead as the physical body. Just as the flesh of the body decays in the physical plane, the astral body decays in the astral plane."

❀

"What about the breath-form and the doer?" I asked. "What happens to them?"

"The breath-form and the portion of the doer go together through a period of unconsciousness," he said.

The *portion* of the doer? I wondered.

"This period may last for less than an hour or it may be many years," he said.

"Does anything happen during that period?" I asked.

"A number of things may happen," he responded.

"The doer may become conscious in a dream without being aware of its identity. These dreams are usually incoherent.

"Or the doer may become conscious of one of the early conditions of its life.

"Or the doer may become conscious in one of the positions which it filled in life and continue going over the acts for a long time.

"Or the doer may wake up as though from a sleep and continue a number of activities either with or without a feeling of identity."

"Ghosts again?" I asked.

"It's possible," he said, nodding. "The important thing to remember though is that, in all these states, the doer lives over scenes only from the life it left.

[52]

"Nothing new is done. There is no new thinking.

"And in none of these instances is the doer aware that it has passed through death or that the world it lives in is not the physical world."

"How can that be?" I asked, incredulous.

"Do you ever ask yourself if you're awake or dreaming, dead or alive?" he responded.

"Not really," I said.

"It's the same way after death," he explained. "The flesh body is dead but the doer is not yet awake or aware that it has passed through death."

"And everybody goes through this?" I asked, trying to get it straight in my mind.

"Everybody," he replied. "These states are passed through by the bad and good alike. Up to that point, there is no reward or punishment."

I shivered. I wasn't sure I wanted to hear about reward and punishment.

❧

"You said 'these states,'" I said to divert him from the subject. "What kind of states?"

His faint smile told me that he knew exactly what I was trying to do.

"In life, a human has many thoughts of which he is only partly conscious," he said. "Then they disappear into the mental atmosphere. After death, these thoughts return to the doer who goes over them.

"The return of these thoughts is the cause of the after-death states."

"How long do they last?" I asked.

"That is determined during the life by the impression which these thoughts made on the breath-form of the doer," he answered.

"But eventually the doer *does* become aware that it's passed through death, doesn't it?" I asked.

"Of course," he said.

"Then what?" I asked, sorry the moment I did because the answer had to be involved with reward and punishment.

"Then the doer wakes and goes over its past life," he answered.

"Mentally, you mean," I said, hoping I was right.

"More than that," he responded. "What it goes over is as real and even more intense than it was on earth."

I don't want to *hear* about this, I thought.

But I had to.

❧

"All right," I said, bracing myself. "The doer goes over its past life on earth."

"Correct."

"How?" I asked. "From beginning to end?"

"No," he said. "The doer's entire life is made a composite and the doer lives that composite. Its acts, its events, its environments are as real as it perceived and felt them to be in life.

"It meets the people it met on earth and speaks and acts with them—and they with it. These are not the actual people of course but reproductions impressed on the breath-form by thoughts of them during life."

"Is this composite life...painful?" I asked uneasily.

He shook his head. "The doer does not, in this phase, go through sorrow or joy," he told me.

"But sooner or later, it does become aware that it is to be judged for its thoughts and deeds on earth."

Again, I thought: I really didn't want to hear about this.

"Before that happens, however," the man continued, "the doer becomes aware that it does not own the form it is in.

"Then the doer and the breath-form separate.

"At which point, all the thoughts that were invisibly impressed on the doer during its life are brought out.

"And its entire life is *felt* by the doer."

I drew in laboring breath.

"You want to stop for a while?" he asked, seeing my discomfort.

[54]

I swallowed. "You're speaking about judgment, aren't you?" I asked.

"Yes, but your own," he said.

I looked at him in curiosity. "What do you mean?" I asked.

"As each thought, act and event is brought out," he said, "the doer is aware that the judgment of them is true—without favor or ill-will. Further, that the judgment is, in fact, *made by the doer itself*.

"How can that be?" I asked. "How can anyone judge himself without favor?"

"Who is more qualified to judge when hypocrisy is no longer possible?" he asked. "When all the mental tricks and rationalizations have been stripped away by death? When only facts can be consulted to arrive at the truth?"

"You mean that we can't pretend any more then," I said. "Can't delude ourselves."

"That's right," he replied. "The doer has no choice but to assess its past life *as it was*, not as it would have liked it to be."

"All right," I said. "I understand. What next?"

※

"Next," he continued, "the doer re-enters its breath-form and immediately is unconscious of the judgment through which it has just passed.

"Then all that the doer had or did in its past life rushes in. The world appears again but instead of being the physical world as it appeared to the doer on earth, it becomes the world in which it *really* was, which the doer didn't know about.

"And a period of suffering begins as the doer enters the first stage of hell."

"*Hell*?" I said, my body jolted by the thought.

"Calm yourself," he told me. "There are, in this hell, no tortures. No fire. No brimstone. No foul-smelling waters. Nor for that matter any of the infernal agonies which theologians of various religions have fabricated. There is no cloven-hooved, forked-tail Devil either."

"What *is* there then?" I asked.

"Suffering for sinful acts and thoughts while on earth," he answered. "The breath-form, on which all thoughts have left their marks, now reveals them one by one.

"As they appear, the doer lives through the desire it had. The persons and objects connected with desires are there. But there is no physical body now, therefore no means of satisfying the desires."

"*Every* desire?" I asked in dismay.

"No," he said. "Normal and moderate appetites do not produce this suffering. Only the inordinate, intemperate, vicious desires which the doer knew to be wrong."

I nodded. "I'm glad to hear there's no Devil either," I said.

"But there is," he replied.

I shuddered. "But you said —"

"The Devil that accompanies the doer through this hell is the ruling and chief desire," he told me.

"Does it...have a *form*?" I asked queasily.

He shook his head. "None of the devils in this hell have forms," he said. "They cry. They pull on the doer. They goad, strain and burn, each according to its own appetite, longing or lust. But they have no form."

"What did you mean by 'sinful' acts?" I asked, thinking, at that moment, that this was the most disconcerting of our walks together.

"Sins against one's own body and against itself for one," he said. "These the doer lives over only as desires.

"Sins against the bodies and doers of others produce a different effect. The doer lives over not only the desires involved. It is, also, accused by the people it wronged."

"For example?" I asked, feeling anxious again.

"Those who inflicted injuries or death by violence or criminal negligence," he answered. "Landlord or employers who caused the degradation of their tenants or workers.

"Rulers, statesmen and party politicians who connived at similar wrongs. Hard or indifferent judges. Those who sinned against the doers of others by encouragement to acts of indulgence.

"All hear the accusations and see again the acts they knew about in life. They see their victims sacrificed to their greed, selfishness and corruption. They also feel what the victims felt—pain, disease, shame, despair.

"This phase of hell is worse than the sufferings of those who wronged only themselves."

"The doers learn what they did wrong then," I said.

He shook his head. "They suffer but learn nothing. They do not repent. They have no remorse."

"I don't understand," I said, almost angrily. *"What's the point then?"*

"The opportunity for learning can come only on earth in the next life," he said.

"The suffering the doer experiences is not for the sake of punishment but to purify the breath-form.

"Punishment is reserved for the next life on earth."

✿

We walked in silence for a while. I sensed that the man was giving me time to assimilate what he'd told me.

This was verified as, finally, he said, "Shall we go on?"

I sighed heavily. "All right," I answered.

He patted me on the back. "I know it's a lot to take in all at once," he told me.

"A bit," I agreed. Then I braced myself for more, murmuring, "I'm ready though."

"Good." He smiled.

"The doer has, so far in this phase of hell, experienced only its feelings and desires," he went on.

"The anguish and suffering from these feelings and desires have loosened the doer from its breath-form once again.

"The doer, now without the breath-form, is no longer conscious as the past human it was.

"It is conscious only as the doer portion that was in the body."

[57]

"You've said this several times now," I told him. "What do you mean by the doer *portion* that was in the body?"

"At any time," he answered, "the doer-in-the-body is only one of twelve portions of the entire doer.

"These twelve portions are inseparable yet each portion re-exists separately. The twelve re-exist successively one after another, in life after life."

I groaned. "That's too much for me to handle right now." I told him.

He smiled. "It's not important that you handle it right now," he said. "There's plenty of time."

"Where *are* we then?" I asked.

"The doer has, so far, in this phase of hell, experienced only its feelings and desires," he reminded me.

"Right," I nodded.

"Now it begins to feel the presence of its conscience," he said. "It knows that it must make reparations for its sins."

"I understand," I said.

"Gradually, another kind of feeling comes," he continued. "This is the feeling of *right* and *wrong*. The doer becomes conscious of the right or wrong of the feelings and desires it experienced and this starts the turmoil over again.

"Now feelings of remorse, repentance and sorrow are experienced. Feelings of duties not done or violated."

"These feelings are, in time and with far more detail than I'm giving you, purified and the suffering ends. The doer has successfully passed through hell."

"Then what?" I asked.

"What else?" He smiled. "Heaven."

☆

I peered at him closely.

"Heaven?" I said. "There really is a heaven?"

He smiled again. "If there's a hell, it's only fair that there's a heaven too."

"I presume that, like hell, it has none of the accouterments most people associate with it," I said.

"That depends," he replied.

[58]

"On what?" I asked.

"Let's discuss the fundamentals first," he suggested.

"When the doer parted from its breath-form, the breath-form rose to a higher plane."

"A higher plane," I repeated.

He could see that I was tentative and said, "The light plane of the physical world."

I stared at him in astonishment. "You mean that everything you've described so far—now to include heaven itself—*is still attached to the physical world*?"

He nodded. "Throughout all our discussions, we'll never deal with any higher plane," he said.

I had a dizzying, momentary sense of planes so high that, even if they were described to me in detail, I couldn't possibly comprehend them.

I had to let go of that. The planes we were already discussing were more than enough to challenge my understanding.

"Are you all right with this so far?" he asked.

I had to smile and make a sound of bewildered amusement. "Oh, sure," I said. "I'm doing fine."

He returned my smile, patting me on the back once more.

"You're doing excellently," he reassured me.

"Okay." I drew in a deep breath. "So the breath-form has ascended to the light plane of the physical world. What does it do there?"

"Waits for the doer," he answered.

"They're reunited again," I said.

"Correct."

"Then what?" I asked.

"The doer, now with its breath-form and senses restored, continues its earth life as though there had never been any interruption.

"*But the life is idealized now.* No sins. No trouble. No sorrow. No poverty. No loss. No sickness. No death. No anger. No greed. No envy and no selfishness."

"Sounds like heaven," I said, restraining a smile.

He chuckled. "Heaven is a state of total happiness," he said. "Everything that could possibly mar unalloyed happiness is absent."

"Loved ones reunited there?" I asked.

"Indeed," he said. "The relations of sweethearts, husbands and wives are there. But idealized, of course. Carnal thoughts were 'burned off' in the hell experience.

"Mothers have their children whom they lost on earth. Friends find their friends. There are no enemies."

"What do all those people do there?" I asked. "Just hang out?"

He smiled. "Doers in heaven carry out the occupations they had on earth."

"But only if their occupations were ideals for them," he added quickly, seeing me about to speak.

"And, needless to say, all occupations are free from the thought of gain through loss by others. Joy lies only in the service rendered."

"Sounds very nice," I said.

He nodded, smiling. "It *is*."

"What else?" I asked.

"Well..." He thought about it for a moment or two. "There is no sleep. No darkness. And no weariness in heaven."

"I presume there's no such thing as eating and drinking either," I said.

"For its own sake, no," he replied. "There may be eating and drinking if that was part of an ideal occupation."

"Such as what?" I asked.

"Oh..." He gestured with his hands. "Such as a mother's or a host's preparations to give enjoyment to others."

"I see." I nodded, then asked, "What does heaven look like?"

"That depends," he answered, "on what the doer longs for. You asked about accouterments that people associate with heaven.

"It can have whatever is desired. Rivers, meadows, flowers. Lights, buildings, heavenly music."

"Religion?" I asked.

"If that's what the doer wants," he said. Doers in heaven can have their religion—but purified from commercialism, bigotry and fanaticism."

[60]

"What about God?" I asked.

"God will be there in whatever form he was conceived on earth," he told me. "Christ and saints and angels, too. All of them will be in heaven as they were believed in on earth."

"If you don't mind my saying so," I said. "It all sounds a little dull to me personally."

He laughed. "Oh, no," he responded. "There is nothing tame, colorless or inane about heaven.

"The pulse of life and enjoyment runs higher than it does on earth."

"Why should it?" I asked.

"Because there are no drawbacks or obstacles to lessen enjoyment," he said. "Joys in heaven are keener and more alive than on earth."

"But what are they based on?" I asked.

"Heavenly enjoyment is the result of what the doer thought or did in the earth life," he answered.

"*Nothing is added to what the doer wished for or aspired to while on earth.*"

"Are you saying that there's no growth then?" I asked. "No learning?"

"No more than in the hell experience," he said.

"The doer learns nothing *new* in heaven.

"*This is the crux of everything. Remember this.*

"*The earth and the earth only is the place for learning.*"

"Is heaven *real* then?" I asked as the question occurred to me, "Or is it just—what? A dream? A mirage?"

"Heaven is not a mere belief," he assured me. "Not just a fancy or beautiful mirage.

"It is, in fact, nearer to reality than anything on earth.

"After the grossness has been removed in the hell experience and the doer enters heaven, the relationships which have remained with it are more real than they were on earth.

"The doer in heaven is in the happy state for which it always longed during its earth life."

"But how can everybody have in heaven exactly what they long for when everybody longs for something different?" I asked.

"True," he said. "The ideals of earth life are, as you say, different for everyone. If they were all to carry out their ideals, that would interfere with the carrying out of others ideals. Then there would be no heaven for the others."

"*How can it work then*?" I asked in confusion.

"In order for each doer to be in heaven," he answered, "it is necessary that it be in its *own* heaven and not in that of someone else because then neither would have one."

"No one ever shares each other's heaven then?" I asked. "They're all *separate*?"

"Not necessarily," he answered. "Each can be in the other's heaven according to the ideals of that other."

"But, in essence, each doer's heaven experience is its own," I said.

"It isn't quite that simple," he responded, "but, in essence, yes, that's true."

"How long does this last?" I asked.

"Impossible to answer," he told me.

"Why?"

"Because there is no time in heaven," he said. "Heaven is an eternity.

"It is not made up of successive scenes and events. Of growing and aging. Of changes. Of beginnings and endings.

"Heaven is a composite of all these.

"For instance, a mother would not see or think of her son as the baby, the child, the teenager, the bridegroom, the father and so on. She would see him as a composite of all these."

"Something occurs to me," I said.

"Yes?" he asked.

"How can there be reincarnation if heaven is an eternity?"

"Good question," he said. "There is an end to heaven for every doer when it has lived out all the ideals it had on earth.

"Then there comes a state of rest without activities and without any appearance of ending.

"Once again, the doer separates from its breath-form as it is in deep sleep on earth.

"And, in this second stage of purification, the doer remains until it is again to return to earth."

"Which happens how?" I asked.

He smiled and patted my back. "Next time," he said.

As though on cue, I stopped and watched him walk away. This time I could not remain silent though.

"*Who are you*? I called after him.

He continued walking, looking back across his shoulder with a smile.

"Everything will be explained in time," he told me. "Be patient."

It was the end of our fourth walk.

🌿 Fifth Walk

"*G*OOD MORNING!" the man said cheerfully. He was waiting for me at the foot of the path.

I returned his smile. "Good morning to you," I replied.

"Ready for more?" he asked. I swear there was a twinkle in his eyes.

"That's why I'm here," I said, still smiling.

"Good!" He rubbed his hands together. "Let's be off then."

We started walking along the path.

"You're enjoying this, I hope," he said.

"I must be," I told him. "This morning I didn't even have my coffee. I just left the house. *Knowing you'd be here*," I added, pointing at him.

"Oh, yes?" he said, quietly amused.

We walked in silence for a short while before he continued. "About your need to know who I am," he said.

"Let's call it more a wish," I responded.

He chuckled. "A wish then," he said. "I just want to re-affirm to you that I'm not being evasive or mysterious without good reason."

"I've assumed there's a reason," I said.

"There is." He nodded. "And, as I've indicated, in time I'll explain."

"One question?" I asked.

"Yes?" Was that a wary smile?

"You're not staying with anyone in the community, are you?"

"No," he said. "I'm not."

"Have you been on the path every day?" I asked. "Or only when you know I'm coming?"

He smiled. "You make me sound omniscient now," he said.

"I'm beginning to think you are," I told him. "Which brings up a second question."

"A third, in fact." he teased.

"Okay, a third," I agreed, exchanging a smile with him. "Does it make any sense for me to ask you how you know all the things you've been telling me?"

"Some day, you'll know them too," he said.

His answer caught me by surprise. How could that be possible?

"Accept it for now and let's go on," he said.

"Yes sir," I responded obediently.

He smiled. "Where were we then?"

I drew in a lengthy breath.

"About to discuss reincarnation," I said.

"Ah, yes," he nodded. "Reincarnation."

"Before we start," I said, "there's a question I have left over from our last walk. I didn't find an opportunity to ask it."

"Ask it now then," he said.

"Regarding those who've died —"

"Passed on is actually a better description," he said.

"All right. Passed on. Is it possible for the living to communicate with them?"

"It's not a good idea," he replied, surprising me. "If anyone tries to communicate with a doer in an early post-mortem state, there will either be an interference with that state or, worse, the interference will actually bring the doer *out* of that state.

"Then the condition in which the doer is automatically living over past scenes will cease and the doer will receive an untimely shock which could cause it to have a longing to return to earth.

"Or it might acquire a fear of earth and go through a period of suffering and uncertainty until its time for judgment comes.

"It's one thing for the doer to try to come back.

"To force it to come back is quite another."

"It *can* be done though," I said.

"Unfortunately, yes," he replied.

"Complete with *apparitions*?" I asked.

He nodded gravely. "There are various kinds of apparitions," he said. "Some have more or less of a connection with a doer. Some have none.

"Some apparitions appear because a medium draws them to his or her body. This is sometimes aided by the thoughts of those attending a seance.

"So a doer, dreaming of one who is present at a sitting, may be attracted to the medium.

"Or, after waking from the dream—before the judgment— the doer may, on rare occasions, be drawn to the medium. To give information perhaps; this is extremely rare. Or to express regret to one who is living. Or to attempt to do something which the doer wished to have done before it departed.

"Or a doer may be attracted to the atmosphere of a medium if the dreams of the doer are of a mean or brutal nature. Or if the dreams are crude and about things of the earth.

"The apparitions caused by these doers often come about when the breath-form of the doers get astral matter from the astral body of the medium and are clothed with that sufficiently to be visible and, sometimes, tangible.

"*In none of these cases is the doer fully awake.* Hence come the confused, incoherent and inane effusions of these so-called 'departed souls'."

"Apparitions are always caused by the doers of departed souls then," I said.

"Not too many of them actually," he responded. "Most apparitions which come through mediums have no connections with departed doers. They are merely astral shells discarded by the doers during their purifications."

※

"How come apparitions are always dressed?" I asked.

"Not always," he said. "When the astral body drifts away from the corpse, it appears in the garment of death.

"Often they wear a white sheet or a shroud because the sheet or shroud was placed over their body and the astral body 'soaked through' the sheet or shroud as it were.

"If burial clothes were used, the wraith appears in them."

[67]

"Are these apparitions...*aware* of their surroundings?" I asked.

He shook his head. "No, they're senseless," he said. "They can't see or hear or make any more contact than a fog or a breeze."

"Are they the only kind of ghost?" I asked.

"No," he answered. "There are apparitions that are seen in some costume worn during life.

"In this case, the doer is dreaming and its breath-form is automatically enacting the dream. The astral matter of living people is attracted to the breath-form and the apparitions are seen performing the same thing over and over again.

"Usually, these specters are not aware of the beholders.

"Another kind of apparition is one which may occur while the doer does not know yet of the death of its body. Before it enters the dreaming state the doer may bring up a memory of something it was set on doing.

"The desire to have it done vivifies the breath-form which may go to a locality thought of and attract the attention of a living person.

"In such cases, the specter appears lifelike and leads the living person to a place where a letter, a document, a treasure or even a murdered or lost body lies.

"This sort of specter is likely to continue its visits and actions until that which the doer was determined to have done is accomplished."

"It doesn't sound, to me, as though communication with the dead is a very practical idea," I said. "Not to mention whether it's a good idea or not."

"Well, it's done a great deal of harm," he said. "It can open relations between the world of the living and the earth-bound and often evil creatures of the astral-physical plane.

"The results of this make the medium an automaton who is possessed sometimes by low, degrading influences, nature ghosts, desire ghosts of the dead and beings which are mixtures of the two."

His words had made me shudder. "And here I always thought that mediumship was supposed to imply some kind of advanced spiritual ability," I said.

"The difference in degree and development of mediums are many," he said. "Generally speaking there are two kinds.

"One remains in control. His astral body and breath-form are trained and his doer remains conscious throughout any sitting.

"The second kind abandons all these things to outside controlling entities and is ignorant of what is done with it while in the mediumistic state.

"Unfortunately, mediums of the first kind are few," he finished.

"It sounds dangerous," I said.

"It can be dangerous," he told me. "The known history of some of those who keep 'open house' for unknown beings, which have then obsessed and controlled them, should be a lesson to those who want to be mediums."

Seeing the look I must have had on my face, he smiled sympathetically. "Enough of that," he said. "There *are* disturbing elements in the after-death states but I hadn't intended to alarm you with them. Shall we go on?"

❦

"One more question," I told him.

"Are you sure?" he asked.

"It's not frightening," I said. "At least I don't think it is.

"*Ectoplasm.* Does it really exist?"

"Of course it does," he answered. "There issues, usually from the side of the medium—a *physical* medium as opposed to a *mental* one—a soft, bluish, phosphorescent, plastic stream which is matter withdrawn from the medium's physical body.

"This stream gives form to the materializing entity, whatever it may be. This may consist of an entire human form or only a head or a hand. One or two or even more forms may be manifested at the same time."

"Only people?" I asked.

"No," he said. "Fabrics, flowers, musical instruments, bells, tables, and other things may also be manifested.

"These things are hard or flexible to the touch. They can actually be examined."

"And they're formed from matter withdrawn from the medium's physical body," I said, trying to get it set in my mind.

"And reinforced by effluvia drawn off from the physical bodies of the sitters," he replied.

"How long can these things last?" I asked.

"For a few seconds or for hours," he told me.

"What determines that?" I asked.

"It depends on the vitality of the medium and the sitters," he told me. "Also on the harmonious wish to have that particular form remain.

"Skepticism, ridicule or disbelief will interfere with or dissipate it."

"It can only happen in the dark, I presume," I said.

"Usually," he replied. "The manifestations can't ordinarily be done by daylight. Sunlight and strong artificial light interfere because such illumination is harsh in its action on this finer matter, preventing its formation and expansion.

"The dark—or soft moonlight or low artificial light— furnishes a better condition."

"You make it sound like stage requirements," I said, smiling.

He returned the smile. "Well, a seance room *is* something like a play," he observed. "A play in which the actors converse with the audience.

"The medium—and, often, the audience—furnish the costumes the actors wear.

"The audience, though unknowingly, decides what characters the apparitions will assume.

"And whatever information is given is developed from such intelligence as the audience furnish."

"Is it *always* a play?" I asked. "Doesn't any information of a higher order come out of seances?"

"It's possible that information of a higher order may be given," he said. "But it's been so rare as to be virtually negligible."

"Okay," I said, nodding, satisfied. "Reincarnation."

"Very well," he said, with a smile. "First let's review the twelve stages that take place between lives."

"*Twelve* stages," I said. "And *twelve* parts to the doer. Any connection to the twelve signs of the Zodiac?"

"Yes, as a matter of fact," he said, smiling again, "but we'll go into that some other time.

"Returning to reincarnation ..

"There are twelve states, stages or conditions constituting one round which each doer passes through from one life to its next on earth.

"Eleven of these are stages after-death in the preparation for another life.

"In the twelfth, the doer re-exists in a human body."

"What *are* the stages?" I asked.

"In the first of the after-death states," he began, "the doer lives and dreams about certain events and scenes of the life just ended.

"This stage may be of short duration or seem to last for centuries.

"At the end of the first stage is the judgment.

"The second stage has to do with the feelings and desires of the doer.

"Eventually, there is a separation of its good from its evil desires. Then a separation from its breath-form.

"This period between the first and the third stage is that which is spoken of as hell.

"The third stage is the grading of the doer's thoughts.

"In the fourth stage, there is a purification of these thoughts.

"In the fifth stage, the doer is purified. The breath-form is cleansed and ready for the doer to use in the stage spoken of as heaven.

"In the sixth stage, the doer is reunited with its breath-form and is in its heaven.

"In the seventh stage, there is a period of peaceful rest.

"It is during this period that the other eleven doer portions re-exist one after the other in succession.

"*Each uses the same breath-form which is common to all twelve doer portions.*

"In the eighth stage, the doer is made conscious of the thought for the next life and the breath-form is summoned to again serve that doer portion.

"In the ninth stage, the form of the breath-form enters the body of the mother-to-be and causes conception. This stage covers the first three months of inter-uterine life.

"In the tenth stage, placental life begins and the flesh body is developed. This stage covers the second three months of the prenatal period.

"In the eleventh stage—the last three months of pregnancy—the human form is completed.

"In the twelfth stage, the body is born into the physical world.

"Here the body grows, its senses become active and it is developed and made ready for occupancy by the doer."

"Talking about 'life after death' as a separate and distinct period from life *before* death really doesn't make any sense then, does it?" I said. "I mean, it's just a segment in a twelve-part circularity, isn't it?"

"Exactly," he responded. "A three-part continuity marked by incarnation, dis-incarnation and re-incarnation."

A question occurred to me and I asked him, "How long does a doer remain between lives before returning?"

"The time between existences varies," he said. "Before a doer portion can exist again, the other portions must have existed in their order, of course.

"But many other factors also influence the period which must pass before a doer portion returns to earth as a human."

"What other factors?" I asked.

"They depend on the needs of the doer portion," he said. "With the parts it has to take in the succeeding life. With the readiness of the world to let it play those parts. With the coming of the other doer portions it has to meet on earth."

"So there's no 'average' period between lives," I said.

"None at all," he replied. "A doer portion may be reborn on earth within a few hundred years or not until a thousand or many thousands of years have elapsed."

❀

"I understand," I said. "What next?"

"I think we've discussed enough today," he said. "We'll continue on our next walk."

I must say that I felt keen disappointment at his words.

I wasn't ready to stop. I wanted more.

It was out of my hands, however, as, with a smile and a farewell pat on my back, he walked away from me.

I stood immobile, watching his departure.

Then, as he turned a bend and disappeared, an impulse struck me and I found myself walking after him.

I knew, somehow, that I wasn't supposed to do this but the inner compulsion was not to be resisted and I strode hastily along the path.

As I turned the bend, I stopped in my tracks, a sudden dropping sensation in my chest and stomach.

The man was nowhere to be seen.

I looked in all directions. No houses were visible. And, all along the path, three-rail fences bordered it.

He could not have moved out of sight so quickly.

I stood motionless, staring along the empty path..

My heartbeat thudding very heavily.

Which was the rather unusual ending of our fifth walk.

❦ Sixth Walk

$\mathcal{A}$s I WALKED from my house to the path the next morning, I vacillated endlessly in thought.

Should I or should I not confess to the man what I'd done?

I felt ashamed of having followed him.

I should have, as on other days, turned back and gone home.

I hadn't though and there was no retreating now from this new disquiet that had been aroused in me.

Who, in fact, *was* the man?

More to the point, I had to confront: *What* was he?

It was not that I was still clinging to the misapprehension that he was just some ordinary man who happened to be walking on the path the day I met him.

Who happened to be on the path every time I went there.

Clearly, he was far more that.

And, equally clearly, there was a purpose to his having met me.

Or, to be more accurate, having allowed me to meet him.

What that purpose was seemed obvious and obscure at the same time.

He was teaching me. Informing me. Enlightening me.

About subjects which, like so many human beings, I had wondered about but never addressed.

But accepting that only left me with a larger question totally unanswered—perhaps unanswerable.

Why me?

❦

The man was not waiting for me at the foot of the path.

Seeing that, a cold bolt of alarm transfixed me.

Did he know that I had surreptitiously followed him and, because of that, had he gone away?

"Oh, *no*," I murmured, experiencing genuine pain.

Had I made a dreadful blunder?

Now when I was really into our walks? Now when I was learning things I'd never dreamed about before?

Now when I was anxious to learn as much as possible?

I began to walk rapidly along the path.

"Please," I murmured. "*Please*."

I couldn't bear the idea that I had ruined the continuation of our walks together.

Sick with apprehension, I walked as quickly as I could along the path. Past the point where the man and I had first met. On and on. To the bend around which I had followed him and seen that he had vanished.

I turned the bend and stopped.

There was no sign of the man as far as I could see along the path.

He's really gone, I thought.

I stood frozen to the spot, staring along the empty path with, I know, an expression of utter despair on my face.

I blinked and started then, gasping in shock.

Where, before, there was nothing, the man now stood.

It happened so quickly that, for several seconds, I lost all sense of reality.

My brain could simply not take in what had occurred.

I stared at the man. Trying to tell myself, for an instant, that he'd been there all the time and I just hadn't noticed him.

The absurdity of that was immediately apparent even to me, as stunned as I was. There was only one acceptable explanation.

The man appeared from nowhere.

※

I didn't know what to say or do.

I stood there, gaping at him.

Slowly, then, it began to dawn on me.

He had chosen this way to demonstrate to me that what I'd done was wrong.

What better way to do so?

I had suffered full measure, thinking that he was gone and that our walks and conversations were terminated. Endured a terrible anguish because of what I'd done.

And all without a single word of recrimination from him.

Did he know what I was thinking at that moment?

I'm convinced that he did.

For, in the instant I was thinking it, he smiled and said, "Good morning."

I swallowed and discovered how dry my throat was. I tried to return the greeting but my voice would not respond. I managed a smile.

Then, as he stood there, clearly waiting for me, I moved forward until I'd reached him.

"Are you all right?" he asked.

I nodded. Able to speak a single word now. "Sorry."

He smiled sympathetically and patted me on the arm.

"Ready to walk?" he asked.

I nodded. "Yes."

Both of us were silent for the first few yards.

Then I had to speak.

"I guess I won't ask you how you did that," I said.

He chuckled softly. "Best not to," he responded.

And there it ended. With me accepting that the man was infinitely more than your average human being.

Of course I might have posited that from all the things he'd told me.

But I knew for sure now.

To my surprise, the knowledge did not disturb me at all.

On the contrary.

It gave me a sense of comfort.

And, I must add, *pride*.

That such a man—or should I be thinking of him now as some sort of *being*?—would choose me to tell all these things filled me with intense gratification.

Think of me as your companion, he had said.

Had I ever received a more honoring invitation in my life?

❧

"Where were we now?" he asked.

I knew that he was totally aware of where we'd been—probably of every single word we'd spoken—but was kindly giving me the opportunity to rejoin our conversation.

"The doer being reborn," I said. "The doer *portion*, I mean."

"Yes." He smiled. "Which, for simplicity's sake, we'll refer to as the doer. When the doer is ready for an existence, it waits, after its eternity in heaven, in blissful sleep.

"Then, when physical time, condition and place coincide with what is predestined, the doer re-exists."

"*Predestination*?" I asked. "It really *exists*?"

"I wasn't using the term with its usual meaning," he said. "Man's destiny comes not from without but *within*.

"*The individual is solely responsible for whatever happens to him*."

"I see," I said. "What about 'time, condition and place' though?"

"Well, you see," he explained, "the time for the beginning of a certain body must be selected so as to allow the cycles of its own life to intersect cycles in the lives of others with whom it is to be connected."

"Are these always *new* connections?" I asked.

"Not at all," he said. "Many connections have been repeated through multiple lives."

"So I could have known my wife in a previous life," I said.

"That doer portion of her, yes, absolutely," he replied. "And the doer portions of your four children as well."

It bemused rather than startled me that he knew I had four children.

"How do the doer portions of people arrange for the conditions of their rebirth?" I asked.

"When they're human beings," he said, "they cause the acceleration or retardation of the time of the re-existences by what they think and how they act in relation to this thinking.

"A human hastens his return by trying to see facts as they are. By doing his duties without hope of reward or fear of disadvantage. By working to achieve his ideal and by having ideals not too far ahead of possible attainment."

"Is it good or bad to reincarnate as soon as possible?" I asked.

"Generally speaking, it's better for human beings who have good will and who work for the benefit of others to come back soon," he answered.

"Their rapid return gives them the opportunity to think and work in order to accomplish something.

"Generally, a long interval between lives is unfavorable. It keeps a doer from the field of action and from opportunities.

"It is also likely to take it too far out of the times to which it's accustomed. To which its thinking has made it familiar."

"And yet you say it can take thousands of years," I said.

"It can indeed," he replied. "This occurs where the conditions marked by physical time do not afford means for unfolding to their dominant thoughts.

"Or a field of display to their talents.

"Or a suitable environment to their virtues.

"Or the existence of people who understand them and are like them."

"Does the doer portion in any particular lifetime *decide* what its life will be like?" I asked.

"*Decide* isn't the right word," the man responded. "Generally speaking, the doer *affects* what the conditions of its new life will be. But clear-cut decision is not involved.

"The feelings and desires with which the doer struggled and which were loosened by its suffering in the hell experience—and which the doer was separated from when it separated from its breath-form—the doer must deal with again when they manifest in a later life."

"Then the doer really doesn't control the conditions of its life to come," I said.

"*Causes* them but doesn't control them," he replied. "Control is determined by the ruling thought of the doer."

"What's the ruling thought?" I asked.

"The sum of the thoughts of the doer's last life."

"That sounds awfully complicated," I said. "*All* the thoughts of a *lifetime*?"

"I know it does sound complicated," he said, "but though the sum of these thoughts may seem numerous, various and hard to coordinate, *the thoughts which underlie them are simple and much alike because they have the same aim.*"

"The sum of all these thoughts determine what will take place in the next life then," I said.

"Not entirely," he responded. "But they do form a sketchy program for the next life. Some of its incidents are determined definitely, others are open."

"When is all this done?" I asked.

"At the moment of death, all the thoughts and acts of the past life are reviewed," he answered. "This confirms the dominating thought."

"I understand," I said, nodding. "Now. Because of this are we born with specific traits?"

"We are," he said.

"Like what?"

"Well, not attainments like professional or business efficiency or mechanical skills," he said. "These are left behind.

"What may be brought over are tendencies, habits, manners, health and temperament. These are not superficial but specific aspects of the doer itself."

"What about specific events?" I asked. "Are these determined too?"

He nodded. "Yes. Not all of them but certain major ones.

"Among the events determined for the next life are the time when life will begin. The race. The country and the nationality. The kind of family in which the body will be born. The sex. The kind of body. The physical heredity. Inherent manners. The chief mundane occupations. Particular diseases. Critical events. And the time and nature of death."

"Good lord," I said. "That doesn't sound sketchy to me. It sounds like *everything*."

"It only sounds like it," he responded. "As I indicated, some incidents are determined definitely, others are open.

"For instance, the ending of life. The year, day and hour are not fixed by any earthly calendar. Calendar time does not apply to the doer.

"The sequence of changes in the doer is measured by *accomplishment*. Predestined events must have occurred before death can take place. And a certain course of action must have been completed by the doer before the next life can begin."

"Does the choice of a family indicate the choice of a *specific* family to be born into?" I asked.

"No. Only the *kind* of family," he said. "Not any particular one. Except on rare occasions."

"You mentioned physical heredity," I said. "How detailed is it?"

"As I said, the kind of body," he replied. "Additionally, the features of the face. And some other characteristics of physical appearance."

"As well as the sex, you said," I added.

"That's right." he nodded. "Of the twelve portions of the doer, six are marked by *desire* and six by *feeling*.

"The male body is characteristic of and is determined by desire. The female body is characteristic of and is determined by feeling.

"The six desire portions re-exist successively in male bodies. The six feeling portions re-exist successively in female bodies."

"I've been a women in some past life then?" I asked, the idea strange to me.

"Everyone has been both male and female," he said.

"Does that explain why some males claim that they feel as though they are females and vice versa?"

"It can," he said.

"How much of any physical or mental trait actually comes from the parents themselves?" I asked.

"Just some of the material used in the make-up of the body," he answered. "The form and features of a person change little from existence to existence. Pictures of the average person taken at corresponding periods of two or even several lives would show little difference."

"Then parents really shouldn't feel that their children come entirely from them, should they?" I asked.

"Not at all," he said. "We'll go into that later though."

I felt a glow of pleasure at that. At knowing that there was much to discuss still ahead of us.

"You mentioned manners too," I said.

"Yes," he replied. "Inherent manners are character in action. They're important indications of the development of any particular doer portion.

"*These native, predestined manners will work themselves out no matter what the early surroundings were.*"

"And occupations?" I asked.

"As I said," he continued, "the chief mundane occupations of a life are predestined. This is so whether a person *selects* an occupation, *accepts* one proposed for him, or is *compelled* to it by force of circumstances."

"Why is this so?" I asked. "Why the occupation?"

"Because the purpose of man's having a particular occupation is to spur on or hold back his development in a certain direction. Occupations are also the means of bringing the doer into contact with those it is destined to meet."

"You said particular disease too," I said.

He nodded. "Certain of the diseases that people acquire are predestined from their past life. Hereditary disease and some that come without apparent cause are among their number."

"You also said the critical events," I recalled.

"The chief events in life are usually predestined because they reflect things from the past that must be dealt with. They are either things wished for or submitted to—or things *unwished* for that can no longer be avoided.

"Among these are events having to do with marriage and offspring, friends and enemies, poverty, riches and sudden changes, honor and disgrace, travels and adventures, injuries and escapes.

"By what it thinks and does, the doer writes the play for its next existence. Earth is the stage on which the doer plays its parts.

"The problem is that it becomes so engrossed in the play *that it believes itself to be the parts*, not the writer of the play and the player of the parts.

"Nonetheless, as surely as there is sunshine and shadow, every doer periodically exists in a man-body or a woman-body. In affluence or in poverty. In honor or in shame. All experience the ordinary and the extremes of human life. Not to punish or reward. Not to raise up or cast down. Not to glorify or demean.

"But for them to *learn*."

"Is this what they call *karma*?" I asked.

"Karma has been variously described," he answered. "As reward or punishment for one's thoughts and actions. As the law of compensation. The law of balance. The law of ethical causation. The law of action and reaction.

"What karma does is adjust the mutually interdependent acts of the billions of men and women who lived and died and will live and die again.

"Though dependent and interdependent on others of his kind, each human being is a 'Lord of Karma' because each one is the ruler of his own fate."

※

"How much variation in conditions is there in consequent lives?" I asked.

"In the course of about a dozen lives, a doer travels from obscurity to rank," he answered. "From lowness and want to prominence and wealth. From simple-mindedness to intellectual power.

"Consciously or unconsciously, man determines that part of his destiny which he will suffer or enjoy, work out or postpone.

"*All receive the destiny they have made for themselves.*"

"Can people actually *remember* past lives?" I asked. "I read articles about that all the time."

"Generally speaking, no," he replied. "The records that the senses make of lifetime events on the breath-form are destroyed before the doer portion returns to life.

"Still, there are instances of persons remembering something of a past life. They don't remember a great part but see only a figure, a street, a room, a valley. The scenes do not follow one another consecutively though there is sometimes a connection between several scenes.

"Beside the flashing up of such inarticulated scenes, there are sometimes memories of events in which the persons are in action.

"Then more appears than mere pictures. The events bring not only the sight of changing scenes and actions but the hearing of sounds and the feeling of pleasure, fear or hate.

"Many persons have some such flashes but even if they cause a feeling, they are not usually felt as memories.

"People who believe these flashes to be memories have a tendency to clairvoyant perceptions.

"Although the old breath-form becomes inert, the impressions are still preserved in the psychic atmosphere of the whole doer and these are sometimes transferred to the *new* breath-form.

"From that transference can be worked out a sense-memory of a scene or event which caused a particular impression."

"It *can* happen then," I said.

"Yes, but rarely," he replied. "Many persons claim to remember past lives even if they have only momentary glimpses.

"Still greater is the number of those who see nothing but persuade themselves that their fabrications are memories of past lives.

"Consider how unfortunate it would be if the situation were otherwise.

"The education of the doer could not be accomplished if the human being could remember its past lives.

"If the doer remembered its past lives it would be conscious of what it had done in its former personalities.

"A person would then carry too great a burden to have any freedom of action. He would be ashamed of his meanness, foolishness, hypocrisy, licentiousness, cruelty and crimes.

"Or he might be carried away with egotism because of the important characters he might have been.

"He might be dominated by greed to acquire again the riches and power he once possessed.

"The memory of comfort and distinction which once had been his might make present hardships unbearable.

"He would be unable to do the duties of the present moment. He might try to run away from destiny or rush *into* it instead of meeting it as he should.

"Knowing the outcome beforehand, he could not be tempted. He would then fail to get the training and tempering of character which overcoming that temptation could give."

"Generally speaking then, a person recalls nothing of past lives," I said.

"Let me tell you what you *do* recall," he responded.

"In all your lives on earth, you have been indefinably seeking, expecting or looking for someone or something that's missing.

"You vaguely feel that if you could only find that which you long for, you'd be content, satisfied.

"Dimmed memories of the ages surge up, the present feeling of your forgotten past.

"They compel a recurring world-weariness about the ever-grinding treadmill of experience. About the emptiness and futility of human effort."

"I *have* felt that way at times," I told him. I think my smile was bitter. "A good number of times," I added.

"Everyone has," he said. "You may have sought to satisfy that feeling with family, marriage, children, friends.

"Or in business, wealth, adventure, discovery, glory, authority, power.

"But nothing can really satisfy that longing."

"Is this kind of feeling always vague and undefined?" I asked. "Isn't there ever anything specific about it?"

"A number of things actually," he responded. "If we look for them.

"The most familiar is the voice of conscience as it warns us about and forbids wrong desires.

"Another indication is that, at times, in critical conditions, one may feel an influx of power and rise above ones ordinary situation.

"Also, in silent moments, one may become conscious of being totally different from the human being which one usually is.

"At times, one may become conscious of things that have nothing to do with the senses.

"On rare occasions, one is illuminated. The present disappears without leaving any sensation and there is a calm, serene and conscious feeling beyond the senses.

"And in very rare cases, one may actually become conscious of an identity which is beyond one's feeling of identity."

"How often does *that* happen?" I asked, my tone of voice indicating clearly that I didn't think it happened very often.

"Well, it's true that the run of human beings make no effort to find out who and what they are," he answered, verifying what I felt.

"Is that why there seems to be so little change in the world?" I asked.

"But things *do* change," he said. "Despite mankind's failures, the education of the doers goes on.

"It goes on though they do not know any more about it than they know about the involuntary processes which maintain their bodies, digest their food and circulate their blood.

"The education goes on whether they wish it or not.

"In the run of human beings, the learning is small, very small.

"Still they do learn a little."

"How long does a doer have to keep learning before it doesn't have to reincarnate any more?" I asked.

His smile was grave.

"There is a long course ahead for the run of human beings before they cease to be human beings and become conscious of being doers-in-bodies."

"At that time, they will do something so remarkable that..."

He stopped speaking and walking at the same time. Turning, he looked at me, smiled and placed both hands on my shoulders. I tensed, anticipating some incredible revelation.

"Until next week," he said.

Then, turning again, he walked away from me.

I stared at him, knowing only one thing.
I would not be following him that day.
It was the end of our sixth walk.

✾ Seventh Walk

THE MAN WAS, once more, waiting for me at the foot of the path, I saw as I approached it.

His point had been made the day before.

I would no longer concern myself regarding his identity.

I knew that he was someone special.

I hoped that, one day, he *would* reveal his identity to me.

But, if he didn't, I would not allow myself to be distressed by that. The message, not the messenger, I told myself.

It was what the man was teaching me that mattered.

"Good morning," I said as I reached him.

His smile was warm and it seemed as though I noticed, for the first time, just how perfect in appearance he was, how flawless.

Odd, I thought, that I had never noticed it before as he returned my greeting and we started out once more along the path.

✾

"You've noticed, I'm sure," he started, "the emphasis I've placed on thoughts and thinking. Of becoming conscious of what one truly is. Of thoughts returning to the doer after bodily death. That we judge ourselves not only for our deeds on earth but for our thoughts as well. That the third and fourth stages of the period between one life and the next consists of the grading, then purification of the doer's thoughts."

"I *have* noticed," I said. "What does it mean?"

"It means that man's destiny is determined by his thinking," he responded.

"For instance, one who thinks about murder, theft or lust will find a way to convert those thoughts into deeds.

"Or, if too cowardly to do this, one can become the prey of others' thoughts which may urge one, even against one's wish, to perform the kind of act which one thought of as desirable but was too timid to execute."

"Does it work the other way as well?" I asked. "I mean positively?"

"Of course," he said. "Acts of goodness, courtesy, service or gratitude do not come out of thin air but are the result of long, continued thinking."

"And the thoughts of others in that case?" I asked.

"Where there is weakness and hesitation at the critical time," he replied, "one may be helped by the thoughts of others and influenced to do the kind act which one had thought of as ideal but was too timid to execute."

"Is there any way of knowing that all these things are going on?" I asked.

"There is but most often they pass unnoticed," he answered. "That is the human problem, you see.

"Because these factors are unperceived and because it appears that there is no immediate, just retribution, it seems that acts do not produce the effect which they should produce.

"Worthy and noble acts often appear to be without reward and mean and unjust acts to be, too often, crowned with worldly success."

"Why *is* that?" I asked.

"Because justice on the physical plane cannot be had at once due to several factors," he said.

"For one, people's unwillingness to have justice done to them. For another, the unresponsiveness of physical matter to thought. Then, too, the cross-currents of various persons' thoughts interfere. Finally, because the time is not ripe for those involved to come together.

"Justice is the giving and receiving of what is right and just according to what one has prescribed for one's self by one's thoughts and acts.

"But people forget the thoughts they've created, for which they are responsible. Therefore, they do not see that justice administered *is* just. That it is the unerring result of the thoughts which they have created."

"You mentioned peoples' unwillingness to have justice done to them," I said. "What do you mean by that?"

"A man can hasten or postpone the consequences of his past thoughts by his general mental attitude and definite mental set as to a certain course of action.

"He may postpone the consequences of his thoughts by trying to ward off threatening events. Just as he is able to postpone a trial in court or an appointment to meet a creditor."

"Does this postponing process make things worse?" I asked.

"Definitely," he answered. "If a man succeeds in postponing what is unpleasant to him, many of the conditions which are due him accumulate.

"Because of this, the pressure becomes greater until finally circumstances act on him and force him to make an opening through which the accumulated destiny will pour it on him."

"And all this can happen *without that person ever knowing that it's taking place*?" I asked, incredulous.

"The law of destiny works in silence and is unseen," he said. "Its course is not perceptible to the senses. Even its results on the physical plane attract no attention unless they are unusual or unexpected.

"Then most people call them accidents; events attributed to chance.

"Or they might be called miracles or the will of God."

"There are no such things as *accidents* then?" I asked, taken back by that idea as well. "Nothing occurs by chance?"

"Accidents and chance are words used by people who do not think clearly when they try to account for certain happenings," he said.

"They see only the outer aspects of a small section of the history of the doer.

"They do not see connections which produce causes. Therefore, they are without an explanation of what they see and feel because of the physical, mental and psychic limitations of their being.

"So they use such terms as chance, accident or providence to account for the mystery because they do not understand that man's destiny is in his own hands.

"The mystery of the world is caused by this separation of cause and effect."

❧

"To assert that the inequalities of birth and station, of wealth and poverty, of health and sickness are the results of accidents or chance is an affront to law and justice," he continued.

"Moreover, to attribute intelligence, genius, inventiveness, gifts, faculties, powers and virtues—or ignorance, ineptitude, weakness, sloth and vice—as coming from physical heredity alone is opposed to sense and reason.

"Heredity has to do only with the body. Character is made by one's thinking."

"How many birth conditions are caused by thought?" I asked.

"As I said," he told me, "from the parents themselves comes some of the material used in the make-up of the body.

"The rest is all created by thought.

"The birth of the body represents a budget of debit and credit accounts created by thoughts.

"The body comes into the world with the desires and tendencies which the doer has transferred to the child through the mother and father.

"And always remember—*always remember*—that any destiny arranged for man is not arranged for him by some arbitrary, extraneous power but is offered to him, made easy or forced upon him *by his own past thoughts.*"

"How can you change that destiny then?" I asked.

"You can't change destiny already made," he said. "This is the field of action provided by one's past thoughts.

"But the *future* can be changed by submitting to the destiny provided. By working out one's duties and changing one's thinking."

"Then the conditions of life are *specifically* provided to give the doer an opportunity to change its destiny," I said, trying to crystallize the idea in my mind.

"Exactly," he said. "The varied conditions of life are due to the desires, ambitions and ideals for which one has worked in past lives.

"Or they are the result of that which one has forced upon others which it is necessary for one to feel and understand.

"Or they are the means for the beginning of a new line of effort to which one's past actions have led.

"I told you yesterday that the features of the face are pre-determined in one's physical heredity.

"Many features and forms of the body are also records of the thoughts which made them.

"Each line is a letter, each feature a word. Each organ is a sentence, each part a chapter. All of these make up the story of the past fashioned by thinking."

"But so many children look like their parents," I said. "Behave like their parents."

"Physical endowments, habits and traits may seem to be clearly those of one's parents, especially in early youth," he said.

"Yet, ultimately these physical peculiarities are expressions of the thoughts of one's previous lives.

"What is called physical heredity is only a *medium* through which one's physical destiny is produced."

❦

"But to return to law and justice," he said.

"As I indicated, law and justice *do* prevail in human affairs.

"But effect does not always immediately follow cause. Sowing is not immediately followed by harvesting. The results of an act or a thought may not appear until after a long, intervening period.

"People cannot see what happens between a thought or an act and their results any more than they can see what happens in the ground between seeding time and harvest."

"These results might take several life spans to show up then?" I asked.

"They usually do," he replied. "Certain circumstances may be faced again and again until people finally realize that these circumstances are, in fact, exteriorizations of their own past thoughts."

"*Exteriorizations*?" I asked. The word sounded odd to me.

"We'll go into that on our next walk," he said. "Will I see you again tomorrow?"

I looked at him startled. "You mean we're already done today?"

"Tomorrow's walk will be a long one," he told me. He repressed a smile. "That is, if you're here," he added.

"Oh, I'll be here," I said. "But I'm stunned that today's walk was so brief."

"That will give you time to review what we've spoken about on our previous walks," he told me.

"Tomorrow's walk will be a demanding one and it will help you to understand what we're going to be talking about if you re-familiarize yourself with what we've already discussed."

With that, he patted me once on the back and walked away.

As I slowly walked back home, I tried to remember what the man and I had talked about on our previous walks.

He had to have a good reason for me to do that.

Unquestioning, I reviewed our previous discussions.

❉

The first thing that occurred to me was how deceptively simple our conversations had been in the beginning.

I'd read an article in the morning newspaper. Odd, how long ago that seemed. Yet it wasn't even two weeks counting the days I'd stayed away from the path.

The article was about the dreadful state of our nation and it had made me very angry.

How could I have guessed that my initial words with the man which had to do with voting and party politics would lead to the point we were now at?

We'd talked about man's sorry history and half-developed civilization.

True, there had been several words spoken about reason versus body. But they had passed over my head as the conversation moved onto capital versus labor.

Always, however, leading back subtly to people and what they wanted, what they believed, what they demanded for their society.

On our second walk, we talked about the concept of democracy as self-government.

Once more, the man spoke about people. About how willingly they played the destructive game of party politics. Declared their desire for genuine leaders yet made little effort to discover and endorse them.

We talked about the Constitution. How it placed the power of government into the hands of the people.

Who pretty much ignored it, preferring to relinquish their power to party politicians; the wolves and foxes, the tricksters.

The man said that the time is *now* for people to govern themselves in order to be able to govern the real democracy our nation—and the world—can be.

A place where men might discover what they truly are.

✻

It was at the beginning of our third walk that the man mentioned our *purpose*.

Told me that we were heading in a specific direction and asked me if I wished to continue.

I know I hesitated for what seemed a long time, sensing that we were done talking about politics and were about to start on a journey of perhaps troubling discovery.

The first step was a big one.

That I am not my body.

That the real me leaves my body in sleep or in death.

I remember saying, "Oh, boy," at what appeared to me to be a giant leap in reasoning.

Only to have him tell me that the progression was inevitable.

I didn't get that at the time. Now I did. Partially, at any rate.

And so he spoke about the body mechanism I—and everyone—was operating.

About the multi-layered atmosphere whirling around my body. Another giant leap for me to take.

About what he referred to as my *doer*.

My true self. Sexless. Ageless. Changeless. Eternal.

About how that self withdraws from the body in sleep in order that the body may be repaired and refreshed for its next day of existence.

About how that self withdraws from the body in death, returning to earth in a different body when it reincarnates.

That one really threw me. Had I actually cried, "Whoa!" at him as though to stop a runaway?

It amused me now to remember that.

I *had* been shaken though. I recalled telling the man that I just couldn't keep up with him.

Still, wavering as I went, I continued.

To learn about the soul. Or, as he called it, the breath-form.

❧

As our fourth walk began, the man told me about the three atmospheres which emanate from and surround the physical body.

These were the fluid, the airy and the radiant bodies, the radiant body also called the astral body.

Then he told me about death.

How it takes place and what happens to the surviving parts of ourselves—the doer and the breath-form.

About our life review and assessment.

Our judgment.

Then our hell experience for sinful acts and thoughts on earth.

First, an actual re-living of those acts and thoughts.

Then a period of remorse and sorrow for them.

And, having gone through that and "burned off" negativity, our next experience.

In heaven.

A positive—idealized—version of life which lasts until the doer has lived out all the ideals it had on earth.

And is ready to return to physical life.

❧

On our fifth walk, after answering some questions I had about ghosts and communication with the dead, the man described the twelve stages that take place between lives.

Then, as he'd left me, I had followed him on an impulse (a bad one) to find that he'd vanished.

※

It was just before our sixth walk that the man convinced me not to wonder any longer who he was.

Penitent for what I'd done, I listened gratefully as he continued to teach me.

This remarkable man who had asked me to think of him as my companion.

Reminding me once again that each individual is responsible for whatever happens to him—or her—he began to describe how reincarnation works.

How the period of time between lives is determined by how the doer thinks and acts in relation to that thinking.

How the sum of all thoughts in the previous life provides a sketchy program for the next life.

What elements of the new life are determined by the doer's thoughts. An amazing number of them, I learned.

About how relatively little parents have to do with the traits and appearance of their children.

About how what is known as karma adjusts the mutually interdependent acts of the billions of men and women who have lived and died and will live and die again.

He told me about the rarity of past-life memories and how unfortunate for men such memories would be if they were large-scale.

And, after telling me that human beings have a long course ahead of them before reincarnation can come to an end for them, he indicated that, when that time came, men would do something so remarkable that —

And broke off at that point.

I supposed that it was something else I shouldn't nurture curiosity about.

※

Our seventh walk was a short one.

But a meaningful one.

My companion brought up—or, to be more accurate, called attention to—his emphasis on thoughts and thinking.

Not really a giant leap, it occurred to me.

More what he had called an inevitable progression.

What I thought about that article.

What people thought—and therefore did—about their country.

Thinking about what we truly are.

Only thoughts surviving death.

Determining what our next life would be.

The law of compensation operating silently, unseen.

Not by accident but because of thinking, because of thoughts.

Recurring lives provided to us so that we may think anew and change our destinies.

I was anxious to begin our eighth walk.

❧ Eighth Walk

"*I*'VE BEEN THINKING," I said as we started off the next morning.

I had to chuckle at the look he gave me.

"I know," I said. "That's good."

"That's *excellent*," he responded. "Keep it up."

"I will," I said, smiling. "But before we start on exteriorization and whatever else you're going to teach me today, I'd like to ask some questions."

"Ask away," he replied, returning my smile.

"I'm not trying to postpone my destiny," I said, only half serious.

That made him laugh. "I'd never accuse you of that," he responded.

"Good." I nodded.

"So what did you want to ask?" he inquired.

❧

"You told me," I began, "that the only attributes parents give the child—prior to birth I presume you meant—is some of the material used in the make-up of the body."

"That's correct," he said.

"That being the case, what exactly is the parents' role in the child's life?" I asked.

"As you've said," he answered, "those attributes are given prior to birth. After birth, the parents' role is, first of all, to nurture the child.

"Keep it warm and dry and well-fed. Provide it with a comfortable and quiet place to sleep. Give it love and affection. What parents have always done when they took their role seriously."

"And beyond that?" I asked.

"To answer that, we should discuss the stages of life," he said.

"More stages," I murmured.

He smiled. "More stages.

"The first stage begins when the infant body comes into this world.

"It is the most helpless of all creatures. It cannot do anything for itself.

"It must be nursed and coddled and trained to eat and to walk and repeat what it's told.

"Then, out of the darkness of infancy, comes the dawn of childhood."

"The dawn of childhood?" I repeated. "Doesn't that happen when the child is born?"

"No, it happens when it becomes evident that a conscious something—a *self*—has come into the body."

"Parents rarely notice this, I imagine," I said.

"Almost never," he replied. "They are not aware that they are the parents of a conscious something, the self, which has taken residence in their child.

"Nor do they know that it has an individual ancestry of character."

"Doesn't this make problems?" I asked.

"Of course," he said. "With growth of the body there will be—there *must* be—a contest between the conscious self and the physical body to decide which shall rule.

"If this conscious self does not learn of its existence and its immortality during childhood, it is not probable that it will learn during or after adolescence."

"How can a parent tell when this conscious self enters the child?" I asked.

"Proof that the doer is in the child is given by the questions it asks and by its understanding of the answers.

"When a child is about two to five years old, it will in all probability, ask its mother or father questions.

"Who am I? Where am I? Where did I come from? How did I get here?

"No other creature can think of or ask these questions.

"For one to ask such questions, one must have been conscious of itself before it entered into and took up residence in the child-body."

"In a way then, we've all been possessed," I remarked.

"You could say that," he replied. "Except that the word 'possession' usually implies an abnormal occurrence. This 'possession,' as you call it, is completely normal."

❦

"I understand," I said. "So what should a mother do when these questions are asked?"

"The mother should be prepared," he replied. "Her mental attitude should be that she speaks to an invisible one who is related to her and who has come to take up its abode with her.

"When I say 'mother'," he added, "I imply, of course, that the father should be equally prepared to answer such questions."

"And if they aren't?" I asked. "Which is practically all the time, I guess."

"If they aren't..." he said. "Well..

"No man or woman who has passed through the partition of forgetfulness by which fortune removes impressions of their past can realize the lost and homesick feeling that cause many a doer to ask 'What am I' and 'Where am I?'

"Nor can one feel the disappointment of the doer in that child when it is given the usual falsehoods as answers to its questions."

"You mean answers that tell the child, in essence, that it belongs to the parents? That they're the only source of the child's existence?"

He nodded. "Yes. The doer *knows* that it is not the body. It *knows* those answers to be untruths.

"Such answers cause it to suspect and distrust the mother—or the one who gave those answers.

"Knowing that what it is told is not so, the doer in the child stops questioning. And for a long time, it suffers from the sadness of its situation."

❧

"What should the mother say then?" I asked. "Assuming she's the one who's asked."

"All right," he said. "She might say 'I'm so glad you're here. Your father and I have been waiting for you. We're happy that you've come and that you're going to be with us.

"I'll tell you about the body you're in and how to use it.

"You've come here to learn about the world and to do many things in the world.

"You'll need your body so that, with it, you can do these things.'"

"What else could she say?" I asked.

"Well," he said, "she could say 'we're going to be great friends. I'll tell you about the things you see in the world and you can try to tell me about yourself and where you came from—how you got here.'

"Speaking to the doer in this way will put it at its ease and let it feel that the mother is a friend who understands the condition it's in.

"Then it is likely to confide in her."

"And if this *isn't* done?" I asked.

"The body-mind will make the conscious self believe that it *is* the body and prevent it from identifying itself within the body.

"*That is what has happened and happens to practically every human being born into this world.*"

"It doesn't have to happen that way though," I said.

"No, it doesn't," he replied. "When the conscious being born into this world begins to ask its parents what it is and where it comes from, it should be told that a physical body was necessary to enable it to come into this physical world. The father and mother provided the body in which it is in.

"Then, by asking the conscious something questions about itself, its thinking can be centered on *itself* instead of on its body."

"Is that all there is to it?" I asked.

"No, not at all," he answered. "The parents should also carefully note the attitudes, attractions and repulsions of the child. Its generosity or its selfishness. Its questions and its answers to questions.

"Thus the character which is latent in the child can be observed.

"Then it can be taught to control the bad and to educate, draw out and develop the good in itself."

※

"The second stage," he went on, "is marked by the qualifying characteristics of independence and responsibility.

"One's work in the world will serve this purpose.

"The doing of this work develops responsibility. To be responsible means that one is trustworthy. That one will make good one's promises and will fulfill the obligations of all one's undertakings.

"The third stage should be the period of accomplishment. For service of whatever kind.

"The education of youth and the experience and learning of human relations should be the ripened maturity that can best serve the community or state in the position or capacity for which one is best fitted.

"The fourth and final stage of the human being should be the period when retired from active work.

"A period for the contemplation of oneself.

[103]

"A period of review of one's past thoughts and acts in relation to the future.

"One's thoughts and deeds can, by thinking, be examined and impartially judged while in life instead of waiting until the after-death state. There, without the physical body, one cannot do any new thinking.

"One can only think over what one has already thought and done while alive in the physical body."

"What you're saying is that, *while we're alive*, each of us can prepare for our next life on earth?" I asked.

"Absolutely," he said. "One's physical body is the testing ground, you see. The means and the instruments by and through which all trials and tests can be made.

"What is thought and done while in life is the evidence and proof and demonstration of what has or has not been accomplished."

"And parents can help prepare the child to do all this in the later stages of its life," I said; more a question that a statement.

"Parents have it in their power to establish the groundwork for the success or failure of these stages of life," he told me.

"I'm beginning to appreciate just how important parents really can be," I said. "Much more than they're aware of, unfortunately."

"Tragically," he replied.

❧

"You know," I confessed, "I must say that I find it difficult to combine what you've told me with memories of my own children when they were babies. I mean...it's hard for me to believe that there was nothing there."

"But of course there was something," he reassured me.

"Cognizance?" I asked.

"Of *course*," he replied. "They were living creatures as we all were and are. Accordingly, infants respond very well to loving kindness. They are capable of distress, amusement, delight. All manner of reactions.

"I am only saying that there is no true identity residing in the child's body until the doer enters it.

"Then, into the living baby, comes a conscious something that is conscious of *itself*, conscious of being *not* the baby.

"But this conscious self cannot explain itself to itself. It cannot identify itself and say: I am *this*. Myself. And the body which I feel is something in which I reside.

"So it asks the questions."

"How can the mother—or father—answer those questions if they were never given the answers themselves?" I asked.

"There is mankind's problem again," he said. "I told you that the mother—or father—should be prepared for those questions.

"But they were at one time in the same predicament. So they forgot and now give their children the same or similar answers as those which they received from their parents.

"They tell their children that the body in which they are is them. What their names are. That they are 'their' little boy or 'their' little girl."

"How long does it take before the doer loses track of what it is?" I asked.

"Not very long," he answered. "Soon it has lost the memory of who or what it was. It is not unlike men or women who have periods of amnesia in which they forgot their identity."

"It must be disturbing to the doer," I said.

"It *is*," the man replied. "The conscious something tries to do two kinds of thinking at the same time. One kind is about itself. The other kind is about the body in which it is and about the people and the world around it.

"It cannot reconcile itself with its body and its surroundings. Neither can it clearly distinguish itself from these.

"It is therefore in an unhappy and confused state."

"Does it ever completely lose track of itself?" I asked.

"No," he said. "For while the body sleeps, the doer returns to a part of itself which is not in gear with the body.

"But when it returns and is again in touch with the body, it is stricken with forgetfulness of itself. It is again befuddled by the senses. By the seeing and hearing of things. By the name of the body which it must assume."

"It all sounds pretty hopeless to me," I said.

"Not completely," he responded. "The conscious something in a boy or girl does become observant.

"It compares and sometimes reasons about what it sees and hears.

"The child notices much more than it is given credit for."

"Can adults ever regain that state of mind?" I asked.

"Men and women cannot enter the world in which the child lives," he answered. "The man-and-woman world is a different world.

"The two worlds intersect so that the inhabitants of both worlds may communicate with each other.

But the inhabitants of these worlds merely *sense* each other.

"They do not understand because a partition of forgetfulness separates the boy-and-girl world from the man-and-woman world.

"Childhood is left behind by going through that partition. Once that boy-and-girl stage is left behind and the man-and-woman and stage has begun, the partition of forgetfulness closes behind them and shuts them off forever from the boy-and-girl world."

"There's no way at all of regaining it?" I asked.

"For a man or woman to be again conscious of what he or she was conscious of as a little boy or girl, sense memory is not enough," he said.

"The man would have to *re-become* and be conscious as a boy.

"The woman would have to do the same."

"Is there nothing men and women can do then?" I asked.

"They must become familiar with the immortal something in them which does not—cannot—die," he said.

"If they choose, they can begin to find their way out of the labyrinth of deaths and births and become acquainted with the knowledge that could be theirs."

"*How*?" I asked.

"We'll get to that," he said. "I must add that not every doer will *wish* to remain conscious of itself after it gets accustomed to the body it is in.

"Many will wish to play the game of make-believe which they see men and women playing.

"Then the doer will let the senses lull it to sleep and forget itself. Dream itself through that partition of forgetfulness.

"Then it will not be able to remember the time when it was conscious of itself.

"When you commence a new life, you are conscious but in a haze. You feel that you are a different and definite something.

"This feeling of *selfness* is probably the only real thing of which you are conscious for a considerable time. You are bewildered, perhaps even distressed by your strange new body and unfamiliar surroundings.

"You wondered before what I meant when I referred to the body-mind," he said.

I looked at him, startled. Was he reading my mind?

Acceptance came immediately. He had probably read my mind from the outset of our walks together.

It neither surprised nor alarmed me now.

"Yes," I admitted. "What is it?"

"The body-mind is the only means by which the embodied doer can function through its senses.

"The functioning of the body-mind is limited strictly to the senses. Through it, the human is conscious only of the world of time, of illusions.

"However adept a doer may be as the operator of its body, it cannot isolate or liberate itself from nature.

"It cannot gain knowledge of itself by thinking with its body-mind only."

"Is there another mind it can think with?" I asked.

"Tomorrow," he said.

"But..." I looked at him in pained disappointment. "What about *exteriorizations*?"

He laughed softly. "We'll get to that on our next walk too."

"The long one," I murmured.

"That's right." He laughed again. "The long one."

I was certainly glad I'd heard the things he'd told me on this walk. Still, if I'd known it was going to delay by another day what he'd intended to teach me that morning, I might not have asked as many questions as I did about the role of parents in a child's life.

I don't think he had to read my mind to know that I was disappointed.

Patting me on the back, he said, "Be patient. All will be revealed."

With that, he walked away from me.

Was it a coincidence that we had just reached the bend in the path where I had followed him a few days earlier?

Was he testing me?

I can't say that I wasn't still curious about him. But I did restrain myself.

After all, what good would it do to see him disappear again?

So I stopped and watched him until he was out of sight. Then I turned for home.

It was the end of our eighth walk.

✣ Ninth Walk

"*W*E'VE SPOKEN a good deal about thoughts and thinking," the man began when we started out.

"By thinking, the doer in every human body creates thoughts. These thoughts are its own prescriptions by which the human is bound.

"Then, at the right time, condition and place, the doer in the human brings about what its thoughts have prescribed.

"Therefore, all that happens to the human for good or ill is of his or her own thinking and doing for which he or she must be responsible.

"The thoughts of one life which have not been adjusted are carried over by the doer to the next life—and from one civilization to another until they are adjusted.

"Every man is an actor in some spot of the world's stage. He is not aware of the preparation made by this thinking.

"He has forgotten the design and the way in which he designed it.

"But he finds himself on the stage and is buffeted, coddled, led or lured by others who are in the same or similar positions as he is.

"How do you suppose this worked?" he asked.

I thought an answer might occur to me but it didn't.

"I have no idea," I admitted.

"It happens because of the nature of thoughts," he said.

✣

"A thought is a *being*, " he told me, "conceived by thinking, with a purpose and a plan.

"It is like an invisible blueprint to be exteriorized as an act or an object.

"This process of exteriorized thoughts is man's physical destiny."

"When you say that thoughts are real," I said, "how real do you mean?"

"I mean that thoughts are *real things, real beings*," he replied.

"The only real things which people create are their thoughts.

"Thoughts are the forms out of which and upon which civilizations are built and maintained and destroyed.

"The unseen thoughts of mankind exteriorize as the acts and objects and events of people's individual or collective lives, creating their destiny through life after life on earth.

"A thought has a system. It has no size in the physical sense but it is vast as compared to the physical acts and objects into which it is later exteriorized."

I had to smile. "I guess I know now what *exteriorization* means," I said.

He nodded and smiled back, then continued.

"The power of a thought is enormous," he told me. "Superior to all the successive acts, objects and events that bring forth its energy."

"Does it work within the laws of nature?" I asked.

"Of course," he said. "The physical results of an exteriorized thought are produced under the laws of physics, chemistry and the natural sciences.

"These laws are actually subservient to the law of thought."

"How many thoughts can exist at once?" I asked.

"Every man or woman has a vast number of thoughts cycling in his or her mental atmosphere toward and away from exteriorization in the physical plane," he said.

"Every thought, once it is issued, endures and appears cyclically, exteriorized as a physical event.

"Every stone, every plant, every animal, every human and every event has a place in the working out of thoughts as destiny.

"No act or object or event on earth *is* a thought, of course.

"But every act and object and event is the *exteriorization* of a thought which, at some time, was conceived and gestated and born through the heart and brain of man.

"Buildings, furniture, tools, machines, bridges, governments, and civilizations come into existence as the exteriorizations of thought."

"The entire physical world is made up of exteriorized parts of human thought.

"Does anybody *know* this?" I asked.

"A few," he said. "But most people do not know that they are bound by the law of their own thinking.

"Nevertheless, by their thinking, all things that are done in the world are done by the prescription of their thoughts."

"That includes our bodies?" I asked.

"Your body is literally the result of your thinking," he said. "Your present body of flesh is an exteriorization of the thoughts of many lifetimes.

"It is a visible record of your thinking and doing as a doer up to the present."

❦

"You said something about thoughts appearing cyclically," I said. "What did you mean by that?"

"A thought, once it is issued, continues on its cyclic paths after the bodily death of the one who generated it," he said.

"It appears in that portion of the doer after death, during the after-death states.

"Its thoughts are the accuser and witnesses that come to the doer for or against it in the period of judgment and the states of expiation and purification.

"As I indicated earlier, the cycles of a person's thoughts determine the length and nature of that person's 'hell and heaven' experience and approximately the time between re-existences."

"And when the doer re-exists in a new body?" I asked.

"When the doer portion returns to physical life and enters new body, its former thoughts continue to cycle around that human," he said.

"What about *new* thoughts then?" I asked.

"Thoughts of the present life is the other factor which acts on a human during his or her life," he told me.

"That factor strengthens or weakens the already cycling thoughts.

"It hastens or delays their exteriorizations and so precipitates or puts off destiny.

"All features of life which are preordained are the result of the thoughts which the human had in his life.

"That human vanished. He or she was centered around the false 'I' which covered the real—but unknown—identity of the doer.

"The new human is also built around a false 'I.' But it is the inheritor, nevertheless, of some of the thoughts and desires of the vanished human from which he or she also inherits physical destiny."

"The ultimate exteriorization of any given thought is all-important in the scheme of things then," I said, trying to understand.

"Not until a thought is exteriorized as an act, an object or an event, is the reality of it apprehended," he responded. "The physical demonstration of thought is the center upon which the doer which issued it is focused.

"Once a thought has been exteriorized, it becomes destiny."

❧

"Yet destiny is something almost no one thinks about," I said.

"Not in its true sense," he replied. "The average man thinks little about it. He feels the advantage or disadvantage of it. It impresses him as acceptable or objectionable. But he does not think about it.

"He acts in consequence of it but not in consequence of *thinking* about it.

"So he misses his opportunity to deal with it and destiny controls him."

"But it doesn't *have* to be that way," I said, caught in a middle-ground between asking and stating.

"No, it doesn't," he told me. "The consequences of destiny are not impassable. Some of them can always be overcome.

"There is always a leeway and it depends on the determination and clarity of one's thinking about destiny.

"One can act freely with or against his or her destiny to the degree that his or her thinking can control his or her actions.

"There *are* purposes to everyone's life with regard to their thoughts."

"What are they?" I asked.

"The first purpose is to let the doer-in-the-body learn what thoughts are and that it is responsible for its thoughts.

"The second purpose is payment. By this I mean a doer pays and is paid in the equivalent of whatever physical actions it caused or permitted.

"The third purpose is the adjustment between the doer and the exteriorization.

"This adjustment must be made with an understanding that a certain amount of suffering is merited and so must be borne willingly."

"And you say that this can be done only when one is alive?" I asked, knowing that we had discussed this point by trying to establish it in my mind.

"Exactly," he said.

"Life in a human body affords opportunities by which the doer may be taught, trained and disciplined.

"Only in this objective world can all doers come together.

"Here other men and women, marriage, work, business, amusements, worship, poverty, possessions, disease, luxury, vice, plagues and war provide them with experiences.

"Here birth, death, youth and age effect them."

"All this is very general," I said. "Can you give me a specific example of how this works?"

"All right." He nodded. "Let's consider disease then.

"Diseases are the slowly accumulated sediments of thoughts which have passed through the parts affected.

"Once one has entertained a thought, it remains in one's mental atmosphere until it is balanced."

"*Balanced*?" I said. This was a totally new concept.

"Later," he responded with a smile.

"While the thought remains in one's mental atmosphere, it moves in cycles and can enter the physical body when the conditions of the mental, psychic and physical atmosphere are favorable."

"Favorable?" I questioned.

"Confronting one's thoughts in order to progress is always favorable," he said.

"All right." I couldn't argue with that. "So what happens when the thought enters the physical body?"

"There is an increased flow of blood to any part of the body in which a thought dwells," he answered.

"When the thought is proper, the —"

I broke in, asking, "*Proper*?"

"Say positive then," he replied. "Just. Right. Affirmative.

"When the thought is of such a nature the balance of constructive and destructive actions of the blood are not disturbed and the sediments of the thought are filtered into the normal tissues of the body.

"When the thought is improper —"

"Negative?" I asked, breaking in again. "Unjust? Wrong? Non-affirming?"

"Close enough," he said, smiling.

"When the thought is of such a nature there is either an increase or a diminution of the flow of blood.

"The increased flow results in a temporary congestion of the part where the thought dwells.

"The diminution results in anemia of that part.

"From chronic congestion comes enlargements, fibrous growths and other inflammatory processes."

"Would that include cancer?" I asked.

"It would." He nodded.

"And from anemia," he continued, "comes a lack of healthy tissue, a wasting away and a readiness of the body to receive infectious diseases."

"Does it always take a long time for these effects to take place?" I asked.

"Not necessarily," he answered. "Sometimes the effect of a thought upon the body becomes apparent at once.

"Thoughts of anger may interfere with the circulation of the blood and cause choking, temporary blindness or stroke.

"Thoughts of passion may use up the body so as to cause exhaustion or trembling.

"Thoughts of fear may cause contractions or trembling or pallor.

※

"Generally speaking, it takes a long time though?" I asked.

"Generally speaking, yes," he said.

"An infection can take hold only when a body or an organ in the body has been made ready to receive it.

"And it takes long, continued precipitations of thought in it to make the organ ready.

"It takes a long time before the sediments of a thought—and the disturbance in the flow of the breath and blood caused thereby—will affect tissue so that it becomes abnormal.

"And abnormality may increase for a considerable time before functional disorder or pain is felt in the body part."

"I presume that this could happen over a period of more than one life then," I said.

"Absolutely," he replied.

"If the history of many an illness were known, it would reveal causes and a course with a long, continued development having many suspensions and reaching over many lives.

"For instance, cancer is not an ailment of immediate growth—even if it appears after a tear or at a point of irritation.

"Cancer may be the growth of thousands of years.

"In the beginning, a little cancer may not be noticeable as such and the person will die of some other cause.

"In the next life, the cancer will be formed again, be more pronounced, a little larger but still unnoticeable.

"So the history goes on, a cancer being formed each time at a critical period in life.

"The last stage is the one in which a malignant growth of new tissue appears at the usual cycle.

"Therefore, old causes, some of which have been dormant for thousands of years, are finally exteriorized."

❦

"You said that every thought has a purpose," I said. "Does that mean that disease caused by thoughts also have a purpose?"

"Of course," he responded.

"The purpose of disease is to purge the body and the breath-form and force the sufferer to learn.

"The purging of the body is accomplished by a process of 'boiling out' when time and condition and place form a favorable juncture."

"Favorable again," I said.

"Do you still doubt it?" he asked.

I sighed. "I guess not," I said. "Though I'm not looking forward to any 'boiling outs' that may be coming my way."

He smiled sympathetically. "Nobody would look forward to them if they knew what was coming," he said.

I grimaced before asking my next question.

"I presume," I said, "that if someone dies of a disease, the boiling out is complete."

"Not necessarily," he replied, startling me.

"Sometimes a disease causes death without all the sediments being removed.

"Then the sediments which remain have to be boiled out again in a succeeding life until they are completely removed. Until that part of the physical body is totally cleansed."

"What does a person learn from all this?" I asked.

"The sensations of disease impart experience and compel observations and deductions," he told me.

"These observations and deductions may result in learning.

"Unfortunately, most often there is no such result."

"And in that case?" I asked uneasily.

"In that case, the disease will recur and the experience be repeated until the lesson which the disease is to teach has been learned."

"I have a question," I said.

"Yes?"

"What about people who get cured?" I asked. "Doesn't that undo the purpose? Prevent the learning?"

"A real cure is the complete elimination of the disease," he replied.

"This does not happen as long as the impression on one's breath-form calls for the appearance of that disease in the physical body."

"What if the diseased organ is surgically removed?" I asked.

"Surgical removal of tissues or organs may stop the pain and the spread of the disease in the current life but it is not a real cure," he said.

"Nor are medical cures permanent because they are not real cures.

"The best that any physician can do is to alleviate conditions and assist nature in the ways of healing.

"But even if the disease disappears from visibility, its immediate cause, namely the indication for it on the breath-form, remains.

"The most experienced of surgeons, physicians and healers know that their efforts are only aids to the processes of nature in effecting a cure.

"They also know that there is no assurance that any cure can be effected.

"Many times, a case which appears simple and promises success cannot be cured. Whereas a case which appears hopeless is cured at once and with little attention."

"What *about* healers?" I asked him. "Don't they get closer to the real cause of an ailment?"

"In the case of a healer who places hands on the ailing body, the finer bodies of the healer guide outside nature into the weak, inner bodies of the sick person and try to start them into orderly operation. This is called magnetic healing.

"Too often though, healers use up their own magnetism and give temporary relief only.

"They should not attempt to force their own magnetism into the diseased body.

"Furthermore, if the motive of the healers is selfish, the results can be harmful to them."

"Can they be successful though?" I persisted.

"As I said before," the man responded, "ultimately, there is a limitation to how much one can be healed. Illness exists for a specific reason. Until that reason is dealt with completely, disease can only be temporarily eliminated.

"By a healer as well as a doctor."

❦

"I presume then that the same thing is true of self-healing by mental means," I said.

"It is," he replied. "Schools of thought which offer quick ways of curing disease by thinking have many adherents.

"Yet if the cure is no real cure and the disease returns after a while—or if *another* disease is brought out when the first one is forced back—and, if in each case, injurious consequences are added to the troubles of the sufferer—thinking by the rule of these schools is inadvisable."

"It *never* works then?" I asked.

"I wouldn't say that," he told me. "It *can* work but only temporarily.

"Because the wrong ways of thinking have mental blindness in their signatures.

"The thinkers assert things to be what they are not and deny that things are as they are.

"They try to think that generally there is no such thing as disease.

"Yet they believe that all disease, though non-existent, can be cured by mental means.

"Still, disease can sometimes be made to disappear by thinking.

"No matter how much a thought may be contrary to the existing state of facts, it can sometimes make the facts disappear."

"How?" I asked.

"A thought that there is no disease, no pain, no disorder but only health, well-being and comfort where disease actually is will stamp an impression on the breath-form.

"This way of thinking can directly efface the previous impressions.

"Sometimes this is strong enough to compel a new impression that there is not disease, pain or disorder and the mental healer succeeds in effecting a 'cure'."

"Which isn't a cure at all," I said.

"Correct," he said.

"Another wrong way of curing disease by mental means is to will that disease away," he said.

"These healers are not as blind to the facts as the first kind inasmuch as they recognize the disease as a fact.

"But their own thinking is the active force behind the cure."

"And the results are the same?" I asked.

"In some cases, no cure can be effected. In some, improvement lasts only a short time. In others, the cure is permanent during the present life.

"But in no case is a real cure effected."

"Are there other schools of thought in self-healing?" I asked.

"There are schools of thought which admit the reality of disease and adverse conditions and attempt to cure them by directing their thinking against them.

"They persuade themselves that there is an abundance of all good things in the universe. That they are a part of the universe and so entitled to their share.

"They declare their share to be all that they desire.

"So health, abundance, success and happiness is theirs if they think it, demand it and continue to demand it until they get it.

"These formulas have in common a belief in some infinite or supreme power and seek to attract from that power what they want.

"They say that by claiming what they want, they *attract* it, that it must come to them.

"So they assert that happiness, power, influence and comfort are *theirs*."

"How often do *these* methods work?" I asked.

"Undoubtedly, these various methods are successful in many cases," he said.

"This kind of thinking is free of doubts and the warnings of conscience. Accordingly, it accomplishes its purpose because it is not aware that it is false and wrong.

"So health, success and business acumen are often the lot of the followers of these schools."

"They're completely false then?" I asked.

"Not completely," he responded. "There are some truths and good advice scattered through the teaching of these movements.

"But there is a limit to results which follow successful desire.

"When the false thinking has gone on long enough, negative results will be manifested on the physical plane."

"Like what?" I asked.

"Fraud, for instance. Corruption. Nervous diseases. Even insanity."

"Oh, boy," I murmured, grimacing.

He smiled at my phrase, then added, gravely, "Another thing to remember is that while it is bad for one to deceive oneself to actually believe the false to be true, it is far worse to treat another by such means.

"For thereby, one teaches the other the practice of self-deception.

"One interferes with and disorganizes the thinking of the other and causes him or her to suffer from the results of this self-deception."

※

"In recent times," the man continued, "a number of movements have come to the fore which use thinking to produce results on the physical plane. To cure disease and remove poverty and banish worry and trouble.

"In all of them, thinking is used with the intent to produce *direct* physical and psychic results on the thinker and in others.

"Some of these movements have grandiose but ill-defined terms for their doctrines.

"Some have, in addition, a religious aspect and vocabulary.

"All of them embody in their teachings some truths and a mass of falsehoods.

"Thinking in all of them consist in deceiving and being false to oneself in thought

"By the use of such teaching, persons often attain some of the intended results.

"But whether they succeed or fail, they cannot too long interfere with the working of the law of thought.

"They can never, by practicing according to the movements, become really free of disease, want, worry and trouble.

"Afflictions, because they come through thinking and thought—even though they sometimes disappear when they are thought at or against—will always return until the thoughts of which they are exteriorizations are balanced."

"*Balanced* again," I said.

He smiled. "We'll get to it," he promised.

"Diseases are slowly developed disorders in the functioning of a physical body," he continued, "and are all exteriorized parts of former thoughts of the doer.

"Disease is one of the last and one of the severest means the law of thought has of enforcing payment and giving notice that there is something to be learned.

"Disease and want are among the chief means of learning from experience.

"Mental healers postpone that learning and work against the development of knowledge.

"There are few greater calamities for a doer than such setbacks."

"And yet it's understandable," I had to say.

"Of *course* it is," he responded warmly. "Where so many persons are ailing and racked with pain, it is small wonder that one who can dispel disease at once or even after a while—and without resorting to treatment by physicians—is widely acclaimed.

"People should, as matter of fact, use every legitimate means to overcome adverse conditions. In the case of a disease, the person should consult a physician or a surgeon and act in the way that seems most reasonable.

"Suffering is not advocated," he went on. "Nor submissive acceptance to adverse conditions.

"If a person wants health, he or she should eat well, exercise and get enough sleep. And, as I've said, utilize the knowledge of the medical profession when it is called for.

"If one wants wealth and success, one should work for it.

"If one wants to break free of an untenable situation, one should try as hard as possible to do so.

"I am only saying that to aspire to these thinkings through false mental means is a terrible mistake.

"As it is to ignore the fact that, sooner or later, inevitably, the thoughts which created these diseases and adverse conditions must be confronted one by one until these thoughts are balanced."

"All right, " I said. "*What do you mean by balanced*?"

"Next time," he replied.

I sighed heavily; almost groaned. "*Really*?" I asked

He smiled, patting me on the back. "Patience," he said.

I looked around. "We're further along the path than we've ever been before," I observed.

"Yes, you are," he said. It wasn't until later that I realized what he'd replied.

"And yet the walk wasn't that long," I said.

He smiled again. "I didn't mean long in distance," he told me.

"*Ah*," I said.

Another smile. Another pat on the back. "Until tomorrow then," he told me.

With that, he walked on ahead. As usual, I stopped and watched him moving off into the distance.

It was the end of our ninth walk.

🌿 Tenth Walk

"WE'VE DISCUSSED the various aspects of thoughts and thinking," my companion said as we started off the next morning.

"Let's talk now about the two kinds of thinking."

"*Two* kinds?" I asked.

"Human thinking is either passive or active," he told me.

"Thinking of one of these two kinds goes on continuously, even during automatic work."

"What's passive thinking?" I asked.

"Passive thinking is the play of desires around or with the body-mind," he said.

"This is the kind of purposeless play that goes on almost interruptedly in the mental atmosphere of the human being.

"Passive thinking is haphazard, unintentional, random thinking which fills nearly all the waking hours of human beings.

"It goes on without sequence, without reasoning, and it changes with each new impression that comes into the body."

"Is there an interchange with other people's thoughts?" I asked.

"There is," he said.

"In the mental atmosphere human beings circulate not only their own thoughts but also the thoughts of others.

"A visiting thought may take something from a person's thought.

"It may impart something to it.

"Or there may be an exchange.

"Human beings sharing in the exteriorizations of other's thoughts.

"In that case, their thoughts are mixed with the thoughts of others. Attachments, dislikes and interests entangle every one of them.

"In this way, doers share parts of each other's destiny."

"If passive thinking takes up all our waking time, how can active thinking function?" I asked.

"Anything that compels attention interferes with passive thinking," he said.

"A sudden noise, for instance or sudden contact. Or remembering something that must be done.

"Active thinking checks and even stops passive thinking.

"Passive thinking goes on continuously throughout the entire life *except* when active thinking takes its place, suppresses or stops it.

"It even goes on during dreams in sleep. There it is kept by memories and is one of the causes of dreams.

"It also goes on at intervals after death."

※

"Accordingly, most of the thinking that people do is unintentional self-suggestion," the man went on.

"Because the large majority of people live by passive thinking.

"This determines their lives.

"Their lives are carried on without much of an objective or a goal.

"Their lives are steered or led into this position by their senses and by passive thinking with these senses.

"People often recognize that extraordinary results are sometimes produced by intentional self-suggestion.

"They almost never recognize that still more extraordinary results are produced by *unintentional* self-suggestion.

"Passive thinking has more power than active thinking.

"It is unobtrusive, unobserved and automatic.

"It accumulates until its mere *quantity* gives it a preponderance over active thinking."

"What *is* active thinking though?" I asked.

"Active thinking is an effort to focus and hold the mind steadily on the subject of thinking," he said.

"You said that passive thinking goes on at intervals after death," I replied. "Is that true of active thinking as well?"

"No," he responded. "Not at all."

"Without a physical body, the doer in a human cannot do any active thinking.

"Thinking after death is an automatic, mechanical reproduction caused entirely by the thoughts which were created and entertained during life.

"As I've told you, thoughts when issued are beings.

"They have a potential system which gives them a certain inherent power.

"They are centers of force.

"They have no form that can be seen, even clairvoyantly.

"But because of the power in thoughts, the entire material world with all its acts, objects and events exists and is maintained and changed."

❦

"Let me go into more detail," he said.

"Thoughts may be conceived, gestated and born.

"Or they may be former thoughts of the same—or another—person which are received, entertained and issued again.

"Usually, a thought conceived and born—or received and entertained—is issued many times before it is exteriorized.

"Furthermore, no one thought can be exteriorized separately from everything else.

"No thought can act independently of its relation to an other thought."

"I don't follow you," I said.

"*Two or more thoughts of the same person* are necessary to bring about an exteriorization," he said.

"Or at least one thought by one person and at least one thought by another person.

"Two or more thoughts *must* touch or cross each other for the exteriorization of either thought or both to take place."

"Isn't that awfully complicated?" I asked.

"Very," he said.

"All human beings are issuing thoughts. Many of these run counter to the thoughts of any one of them.

"The difficulties presented in the case of one man or woman are multiplied when the thoughts of others—or those of all the people living in the world—or those of *all human beings who have ever lived*—are to be considered.

"Good lord," I muttered. The concept boggled my mind.

"Another factor is that, out of the millions of thoughts—one's own and those of others—only a small number can be realized in the physical world at any one time."

"A question," I said.

"Yes?"

"Can the exteriorization of a thought be stopped? Delayed? I mean once it's begun?"

"A thought can be revoked, dissipated or changed *before* it becomes exteriorized," he answered. "But once it's been exteriorized, it continues until it's balanced."

I didn't respond to that, assuming that, at last, he was going to explain *balanced*.

He didn't, continuing with his description.

"If the one who issued this thought dies, the thought—as I've indicated—goes with the doer and influences the building of the new body.

"In that new life and in subsequent lives of the doer, the thought continues to cycle and to bring about *another* exteriorization or exteriorizations until the thought is balanced."

Again, I thought. Would he explain it *now*?

Again, he didn't and I held my tongue. I assumed that he'd explain it when it was time. He'd said that he would.

"Again in reference to thoughts, not their exteriorization," he continued. "Some thoughts are revoked before they are issued.

"This is so if the doer has disapproved of the thought and its purpose after the thought has been generated.

"When the doer refuses it exteriorization, it is dissipated.

"The reason may be fear of discovery or of the consequences.

"Or it may be change of aim.

"Some thoughts are *changed* before they are exteriorized. The change occurs when the aim in the thoughts is changed.

"With regard to the revoking of a thought, if the dissolution took place because the doer recognized and respected conscience, the mental atmosphere is improved and a tendency to reject similar thoughts is strengthened.

"Where the dissolution is brought about because of fear or expectation of some advantage, the mental atmosphere is vitiated and ready to entertain a similar thought in the future.

"Making the balancing of thoughts all the more difficult, you see," he finished.

Abruptly, he was silent and I looked over.

He was smiling at me with amusement.

"You're being very patient," he said. "But you're *dying* to know what balancing a thought means, aren't you?"

I laughed. "I swore I'd wait," I told him.

He patted me lightly on the head. "Patience is rewarded," he said.

"The law of thought is this:

"*Everything existing on the physical plane is an exteriorization of a thought which must be balanced through the one who issued the thought, in accordance with his or her responsibility and at the conjecture of time, condition and place.*"

"*This law of thought is everyone's destiny.*"

"Thoughts when born contain four factors," he continued.

"An aim. A plan or design. An effect or effects of the design. And a balancing factor.

"This balancing factor is related to conscience.

"A human balances a thought when he performs a duty willingly and intelligently without attachment to the results.

"He may not know about the thought or the method by which he balances it.

"Nevertheless, the thought is balanced by him.

"The important thing for the doer to do, after it has created a thought, is to desire to balance it.

"Balance it with any physical event which is an exteriorization of the thought."

"How is this done?" I asked

"A thought cannot be balanced without payment being made and the account settled in connection with that particular thought.

"For instance, the payment might be made in pain, sorrow terror or despair—for payment is always made in *psychic* coin."

"This is the sticking point, isn't it?" I said, already knowing the answer.

"Yes, it is," he said gravely.

"Man's desire is usually for comfort, possession, luxury.

"But when desire wants rightness to correct it and reason to guide it, a great change occurs in the working of the doer."

"And this more elevated desire takes place through conscience?" I asked.

"Man is informed of his responsibility not by reason but by direct warning from his conscience," he said.

"What exactly *is* conscience?" I asked.

"From learning many things and seeing them verified," he replied, "the doer acquires a certain amount of knowledge of what is right.

"This amount of knowledge is the conscience."

"Can you be a little more specific?" I asked.

"All right," he agreed. "Conscience represents the sum of knowledge, acquired by the doer on any moral subject.

"It is, basically, a sum of knowledge as to *what should not be done.*

"Simply expressed: *Right* is what to do. *Wrong* is what not to do.

"What to do and what not to do are the all-important problems of thought and act in each individual human life.

"*What to do and what not to do constitute the entire public and private life of mankind.*"

"Is conscience the 'still, small voice' that people talk about?" I asked.

"It has been called that, yes," he replied. "It is the ever-present counselor and judge that speaks in the heart.

"It speaks of rightness and reason. Of law and justice.

"Without conscience man would be little more than an animal."

※

"Before permitting the desires which urge, pull and press in on a person, which appeal for or demand their objects, one should listen to the voice of conscience or consider the advice of reason.

"Otherwise, one will act on impulse in responding to the desires which are the strongest claimants.

"*Whatever* one does, one thereby prescribes the law which will be administered to one in the near or distant future as one's destiny."

"And if one *does* listen to the voice of conscience," I said, "what should one listen *for*?"

"The call to duty," he answered.

"*Duty*?" I asked.

"Duty is the one thing man has to go by," he said. "He can always know the duty of the moment if he looks for it.

"And if he does that duty willingly, he either balances or prepares for balancing the thought of which the duty is part of the exteriorization.

"One need never be in doubt about one's duty.

"Conscience will show one what not to do. Reason will show one what to do.

"And thinking will confirm this inner voice if one will listen to it and not to on-rushing desires."

"What if a man commits a wrong and doesn't *know* it's wrong?" I asked.

"A man is responsible to the degree of his knowledge in a given situation," he answered.

"And to the degree of his ability to perform the duties of that situation.

"A man's act is a sin not because he does not know better but because he does what he knows to be wrong.

"Acts done without knowing that they are wrong are not sins though harmful results may follow.

"If thoughts are done with the intent of producing the result, they are sins.

"If not, they are done in ignorance."

"Are all sins directed at others?" I asked.

"No," he replied. "As I've mentioned, there may be sins against one's own body as well.

"Acts by which the body's well-being and usefulness are interfered with.

"These might be sexual over-indulgence. Over-feeding or eating unwholesome food. Drunkenness. Uncleanness. Not taking care of one's eyes, teeth or any part of the body. Not attempting to cure disease once it is noticed. Inflicting a personal injury or the murder of one's own body."

"I can understand the murder of one's own body being considered a sin," I said. "But *over-eating*? Not taking care of one's *teeth*?"

"These acts exist at relative levels, of course," he explained, "but they are all 'crimes,' if you will, against one's self."

"What *about* suicide?" I asked. "You never mentioned it when you were telling me about the after-death experience."

"Well, first of all," he said, "it is not the escape that people who commit suicide think it is.

"By committing suicide, one does not escape from the allotted span of life or from the sorrow, dread, pain or disgrace one feared to endure by living on.

"Death by one's own hand is not like the ordinary case of dying.

"In the case of self-murder, the doer remains with the breath-form in the radiant state of the physical plane.

"There it experiences all it dreaded to meet in life.

"It does not go into after-death states until after the allotted span of life ends.

"In the next life on earth, one will have the same inclination to commit suicide but coupled with that will be a dread of it.

"Most importantly though for men and women to realize, *in no case can one escape by suicide that which one feared to suffer*.

"The conditions from which one sought escape will confront one again because they are exteriorizations of one's own thoughts."

※

"As to sins against others," he said.

"Many *more* sins which will demand serious discipline and retribution are inflicted indirectly upon the bodies of others.

"I mentioned a few of these earlier when we were discussing after-death states.

"Additional sins against others are the manufacture of adulterated foods and drinks or of narcotics.

"Sins of indifference or intent which cause overcrowding, disease and squalor in miserable dwellings.

"Sins of employers who do not provide safe and sanitary places to work and who pay insufficient wages.

"These sins may also be chargeable to those who are not directly involved as employers but are their agents.

"And to persons in public office through whose connivance such conditions are allowed to exist.

"Equally so, *the people at large* are responsible if they know of such facts and do not do what they can to remedy conditions by which these sins are committed.

"In this way, a community as well as its party politicians may commit sins against the bodies of others."

"And sins against the minds of others?" I asked.

He looked at me.

"I think that, by now, you know the answer to that," he replied.

❧

We walked in silence for a while.

So long, in fact, that I turned to him, wondering why he had stopped speaking.

"Is there more?" I finally asked.

He smiled. "There is always more," he said. "I'm just considering whether I've told you enough for now."

I wasn't sure what he meant and made no reply.

"Summing everything," he continued. "By thoughts and their exteriorization the destiny of men and nations is created.

"Not as individuals would have it but by an overall management whose ultimate plan is to obtain a balance of thoughts by means of acts and events.

"Events continue to come to a person until, through exteriorization, he or she pays for past exteriorizations, learns the lessons required by the stage of his or her growth, gets a certain amount of knowledge and so balances the thoughts which caused those events.

"The *physical* events which occur to one may or may not be exteriorizations of one's own thoughts.

"But the *psychic* events—the feelings of joy or sorrow which one experiences from each and every event of one's own life— *are* the results of one's thinking."

"So then," I said, "this constant challenge to every man and woman to listen—or not listen—to their consciences and to balance—or not balance—their thoughts comprises their destiny."

"Well said," he told me.

"If men and women would learn from experience, they would not have to have the same experience over again.

"Unfortunately, men and women will *not* learn from their experiences and so continue in the same round of thoughts and have the same experiences in life after life.

"The good and the evil thinking that men have done remains with them in their mental atmosphere until it is removed by thinking.

"Their acts, good or bad, do not remain. What remains is the thinking of them.

"In their mental atmosphere, there is an immense amount of debit and credit to the account of each doer."

※

"Could you tell me a little more about accidents?" I asked. "I'm not sure I understand fully."

His smile told me that he knew what I was doing. Disturbed by the idea that our walk might be drawing to a close, I was trying to extend it.

He said nothing of that, however, patiently explaining accidents once more.

"An accident is like any other event on the physical plane," he said. "A thought in a certain part of its course.

"As I told you, a thought, when issued, has in it an aim, a potential design and balancing factor.

"This balancing factor, like the needle of a compass, points to the final balance of the thought as a whole.

"The thought endures until the balancing factor has brought about an adjustment through the one who issued the thought.

"Whenever the thought, moving in its course, approaches the physical plane, it causes the one who issued it to be in place for an exteriorization of that thought.

"But the laws which control the exteriorization do not always fit in with the intention or expectation of the person concerned.

"The exteriorization is then called an accident.

"The exteriorization makes visible that part of the thought which touches the physical plane and is not yet balanced.

"Accidents, therefore, come only to those whose thoughts are partially exteriorized to them.

"An accident presents, to the one to whom it happens, something of his or her past, either distant or recent."

"Why an *accident* though?" I asked. "Why not the same lesson presented through some *ordinary* event?"

"Because there is, in the happening of an accident, a special call for attention," he answered.

"An accident rather than an ordinary event produces this call because the accident is unlooked for, startling.

"Also, an accident is the easiest way to bring about the juncture of time, condition and place for the exteriorization."

"Is there any way to avoid accidents?" I asked.

"In the overall sense, no," he responded. "But an attitude of willingness to perform one's duty will allow destiny to come in its natural order, without postponement or hastening."

"*Hastening*" I asked in surprise.

"An attitude of fear may precipitate destiny," he told me. "It may anticipate and project what would otherwise not have happened then."

With that, he patted me on the back and said quietly, "Our walks are at an end now."

❀

"*What*?" I felt disbelief at his words.

He smiled at my reaction.

"You said *walks*?" I asked. I couldn't believe it.

He nodded. "Yes."

"But..." I wanted to protest but didn't know how. "That's *all*?" I asked.

"*For now*," he answered.

For now. The words echoed strangely in my mind.

Still, I felt astonishment, distress.

"You've told me *everything*?" I asked.

He laughed. "Far from it," he said. "I've given you only basic information. There are many, many things I haven't told you. Things too complex to be dealt with at this time."

At this time. Those words echoed in my mind as well. What was he implying?

I didn't know how to ask. Or what to say. I walked beside him in stricken silence.

He'd said our walks were at an end. Yet he continued walking with me.

Was he giving me time to adjust to what he'd said?

"The things you *have* told me though," I said, words finally coming to me, "will they go on forever?"

"Unless men find the way." he answered.

"The way?" I asked.

"A way of thinking for the development of the human mind," he said.

"How can they find it?" I asked.

"This way of thinking can only begin when humans inquire into the causes of human action and inaction," he said.

"When they inquire into the purpose of living.

"The purpose of health and disease. Riches and poverty. Virtues and vices. Life and death.

"Then men will discover the futility in human effort for the things of the world.

"Discover the vanity and the emptiness of such life.

[137]

"Discover that no human possession is worthwhile.

"But these discoveries can only be made when humans have reached the saturation point of human experiences.

"Then, by a flash of interior light, men will see the world as it is.

"See that the objects and situation which men desire revolve.

"That they have appeared and disappeared to them many times.

"They will see that these things are toys which attract people and hold the attention and interests in life.

"See that one set of toys gives place to another.

"The discovery of the futility of such effort and the state of emptiness that follows will eventually force men to question who they are and to search into the recesses of their beings for a way out of the emptiness.

"So men will become conscious that there is a way and that they desire to find it."

"And then?" I asked.

"The period from the time when men first discover the futility of human effort for the things of the world to the time when they enter the way will see many changes in their environment, in their occupations, in their associations and in their physical bodies."

"Changes in their *bodies*?" I asked, startled.

"I began to tell you about this at the end of our sixth walk," he told me. "Then I decided against it. It's too complex for us to talk about now."

Now again. Did it mean what I thought it did? What I hoped it did?

I put the notion aside. "What about the rest then?" I asked.

"Men's surroundings, their work and their ties will change naturally as their thinking changes.

"Men live in a certain environment and are held by various ties and duties to locality, nation, race, friendship, family, marriage and position.

"These ties cannot be deliberately broken. They must be worn away or must fall away.

"Even possessions should not be done away with merely for the sake of getting rid of them.

"Men have them for a purpose.

"They mean responsibilities and trust and men must answer for them and their stewardship.

"Possessions will disappear naturally if they are in the way of man's advance."

"If all these things have worn or fallen away," I said, "is there any way of telling whether any particular man has started along the way?"

"None," he replied. "There is no outward condition, no mark or criterion by which the world can distinguish from the run of human beings one who made the great discovery and has made the choice for an inward life.

"As a person progresses by thinking, that person will gradually retire from the world inconspicuously and without attracting any attention."

"I presume you're one of them," I said.

He only smiled, continuing.

"The states through which one passes before reaching the psychic standard to enter the way vary with different persons," he said.

"But the standard to which each person must have attained are substantially the same for all.

"*Honesty and truthfulness* must be the foundation of one's character.

"Ingratitude, malice, rancor, hatred, envy, anger, vindictiveness, jealousy, meanness, deceit, hypocrisy, arrogance, greed, gloom, despondency, fear, cowardice, and cruelty must be strangers to one.

"One must be honest, self-restrained, self-contained and modest.

"That's all mental," I said. "Are there physical requirements as well?" I was thinking again of what he'd said about changes in the body.

"The body must be healthy and strong," he said. "One should be temperate and shouldn't eat too little or too much. Beverages must be free of alcohol. The body must not sleep too much or too little. It must not be abused by fasting or any other kind of asceticism.

"In brief, the body must not be governed from without by nature but from within by thinking."

My sigh was a heavy one.

"By these standards, I have a long way to go," I said. "A *long*, long way to go. I wonder if I'll ever make it."

"Everyone makes it eventually," he told me.

"Man makes the laws for his own future destiny by his own thoughts and acts.

"And by his thoughts and acts, man helps to determine the laws of the land in which he lives.

"Which brings us back to politics," he said.

"It isn't enough to say that real democracy should be achieved in order to provide an environment in which man can discover his true self.

"If man does *not* discover his true self, real democracy will not only not be achieved but civilization may not survive long enough to *see* it achieved.

"The United States of America was set apart to try out self-government by the people.

"They have been led to success in their various wars, their political institutions and their economic undertakings.

"In peace and in war, their escape from the natural consequences of their selfishness and indifference is striking.

"*But this protection and success may not last.*

"There must be an accounting for all that these people tolerated and did in violation of their great responsibility.

"The bigots, the slave traders and owners, the oppressors of the Indians, the political and other corruptionists will at some time meet and suffer at the reckoning which is sure to come.

"The people of this country and the world at large, must give evidence of wakening to their responsibilities in life.

"They must understand that, as they desire independence, so, also, do the people of other countries desire independence.

"They must awaken to the fact that independence, as individuals and as people, is dependent on their responsibility.

"*Independence and responsibility are inseparable.*"

"In essence, isn't that what we've been talking about all along?" I asked. "Self-responsibility?"

"Just that," he said. "*Self-responsibility* is what all men must achieve in time."

※

"It's quite a challenge," I said somberly. "Not a hopeless one, I trust."

"No, not at all," he said. "I wouldn't want to leave you with a sense of hopelessness."

He's leaving me, I thought despairingly.

"What I want to leave you with is this," he said.

"Man's existence on this earth has a purpose.

"There is a *meaning to life*.

"There is, in man, a faith that somewhere in the world—notwithstanding all the seeming injustice—there is, though unseen and not understood, *justice*.

"This inherent faith in justice is part of the intuition which persists in the heart of man despite the adverse conditions which harden him.

"This intuition is the underlying knowledge that man will live through the seeming injustice imposed upon him.

"Live to right the wrongs which he has done.

"This intuition is the underlying knowledge that man is not alone. That a voice within him speaks to him if he will listen. Telling him this:

"You need not feel alone.

"Wherever you are, your higher self is with you.

"This higher self will protect you if you will allow yourself to be protected.

"This higher self is ever ready for your return to it however long it may take you to find and follow the path back."

"To *what*?" I asked.

"To consciousness," he said.

"*Consciousness*?"

"Consciousness is the greatest and most profound of all mysteries," he told me. "The ultimate and final reality. Mystery of all mysteries, it is beyond man's comprehension."

"If we can't comprehend it," I said, "how can we ever get back to it?"

"You must remember," he said. "Only a small portion of this immense universe is familiar to the human. That is, the physical, visible portion which is the solid state of the physical plane of the human physical world.

"Beyond this state, the ordinary human does not even think."

"How can I know it exists then?" I asked.

"You'll have to take that on faith for now," he told me.

"Are *you* aware of it?" I asked.

"I have been conscious of it," he replied.

"I envy you," I told him.

"No need," he said.

He lay his hand on my shoulder and looked steadily into my eyes.

"One day you *will* be me," he said.

I looked at him in shock. "What?" I murmured.

He smiled at me. "What I am," he told me, "you will, one day, be. I was you at this time. And, at some future time, when you have grown spiritually, *you will be me*, your breath-form altered, your physical body completely different."

"You're from the future then?" I asked in astonishment.

He nodded. "The very distant future," he answered.

I felt awe-struck, numb. "How long will it take me to...be you?" I asked; I could barely say the words.

"Perhaps a hundred lives," he said. "Perhaps a thousand. Perhaps a hundred thousand. It's not for me to let you know that. It is for you to achieve. As, one day, you will. As, one day, all men and women will, all men and women *must*."

"*How*?" I asked dazedly.

He smiled again. "The answer to that would take at least another ten walks," he said.

"And when I've done this," I asked, "will I go back and talk to the me that exists today?"

His laugh was soft. "That may well be," he answered. "Since all is circularity."

❁

I blinked.

I was alone on the path.

I looked around in blank confusion.

The man was gone.

I wavered, had to stumble to a fence and hold on to the top rail, trembling at the memory of his words.

One day I would be him.

My mind staggered beneath the weight of that idea.

I walked home slowly to my house and sat on my chair, still feeling dazed. Wondering if I would ever see the man again.

Take those other ten walks with him. Learn what he had not told me on these ten walks.

I sat immobile in my chair.

Thinking.

It's time to begin the search.

Time to take the first steps of that long journey home.